THE SPEED MERCHANTS

THE SPEED MERCHANTS

BY MICHAEL KEYSER

A Rutledge Book
Prentice-Hall, Inc.
Englewood Cliffs, N.J.

Fred R. Sammis: *Publisher*
John Sammis: *Associate Publisher*
Doris Townsend: *Editor-in-Chief*
Allan Mogel: *Art Director*
Jeanne McClow: *Managing Editor*
Jeremy Friedlander: *Associate Editor*
Gwen Evrard: *Associate Art Director*
Arthur Gubernick: *Production Consultant*
Annemarie Bosch: *Production Manager*
Margaret Riemer: *Editorial Assistant*
Sally Andrews: *Editorial Assistant*
Robert Thornton: *Editorial Layout*

Photography Credits

All photographs are by Michael Keyser except those identified below.

Hal Crocker: 15 top, 19 bottom, 22, 23, 27–30, 31 bottom, 42, 44, 46, 47, 49, 50, 52, 57, 59, 60 top left and top right, 62, 63, 65, 66 left, 67, 69 top and bottom left, 71, 73 left, 75 bottom, 77 top right and top left, 78 top, 86, 96, 102, 104, 105, 110, 113, 115, 151 top, 153 top, 155 bottom, 161 bottom, 165 top, 171, 172 top.

Kevin McCarthy: 174.

Balfi Walker: 10, 17, 18, 21, 32, 35 bottom, 40 top, 41, 51 top, 54, 60 bottom, 70 bottom, 72, 77 bottom, 83, 88–90, 93–95, 97, 99, 103, 109 top, 111 top, 118, 120–22, 124, 126, 127 top, 128, 129, 132, 133, 135, 136, 140, 145–47, 152, 153 bottom, 154, 155 top, 156, 157, 158 bottom, 159, 160, 162, 164, 165 bottom, 167 bottom, 169, 172 bottom, 175.

Color

Hal Crocker: 16H top.

Hunter Farnham: 81A, 81B bottom right, 112B, 112D top, 112F bottom left, 112G, 144H top right.

Kevin McCarthy: 112H bottom, 144A.

Kim Milliken: 144P.

Balfi Walker: 16A, 48D, 81F right, 112D bottom, 144F, 144H top left and bottom, 144L top, 144N.

Jacket: Front—Balfi Walker; back—Michael Keyser.

Darkroom and technical consultant: Sioux Iglehart

Copyright 1973 in all countries of the International
Copyright Union by Michael Keyser
Prepared and produced by The Ridge Press, Inc.–Rutledge Books Division, 17 East
45th Street, New York, N.Y. 10017
Published in 1973 by Prentice-Hall, Inc., Englewood Cliffs, N.J.
Library of Congress Catalog Card Number: 73-81314
ISBN: 0-13-833855-8
Printed in Italy by Mondadori, Verona
Prentice-Hall International, Inc., London
Prentice-Hall of Australia, Pty., Ltd., North Sydney
Prentice-Hall of Canada, Ltd., Toronto
Prentice-Hall of India Private Ltd., New Delhi
Prentice-Hall of Japan, Inc., Tokyo

CONTENTS

INTRODUCTION

The Marquis de Portago was a young man of the Spanish aristocracy. He was a superb horseman, the only foreign member of an exclusive British hunt club, played excellent polo, was a fine marksman, and drove fast cars in races. There had been a race in Italy, one that is no longer held, in which cars raced a thousand miles up the length of the Italian peninsula. The Mille Miglia was a mad affair. They say the marquis stopped his car—in the middle of the race—to jump out and kiss a girl who stood at the side of the road. A hundred miles farther on, the marquis was killed in an accident.

There was an eccentric Polish peer, Count Szborowski, who lived in England and raced the cars he bought and prepared. Under wild urging he built immense cars, powered by Rolls-Royce airplane engines. He called them Chitty-Chitty-Bang-Bangs and had some success racing them. The count was killed when during a race his cufflink (his cufflink!) became entangled with the steering mechanism. The cufflinks were a set his father had worn—and had been wearing when *he* was killed at the wheel of a car.

Almost as soon as they were invented, cars were being raced. Racing has become, in a certain sense, the quintessential twentieth-century sport, the sport that grew up as the cars grew up.

In the beginning the cars in America were racing around disused horse-racing tracks, which gradually led to the development of oval-track racing in America. Indianapolis is the prime example of this kind of racing. In Europe, for the most part, early racing was done on public roads that were closed for the day of the race. These public roads were the forerunners of the European tracks, with curves, esses, and chicanes. Cars have raced any place where more than two of them could fit—through the Bois de Boulogne in Paris, along the beach at Daytona, through the mountains of Sicily along the Circuito della Madonie (the famed Targa Florio), along the roads of a great resort, Spa-Francorchamps, through the city streets of Monaco. Some of these races are still run. But motor racing has changed immensely since its beginnings.

It used to be that any playboy wealthy enough to buy a Bugatti, hire a mechanic, and drive to a road where a race was being held had an equal chance of winning—or killing himself. All that was really required was money and nerve. Manufacturers of cars realized almost from the beginning what a grip these men and their machines had on the public imagination and began racing teams of cars themselves. Gradually the sport changed; the men skilled enough to win began to get the support of the factories and were given the best-prepared cars. The grand gesture, the kiss by the side of the road, the leather-helmeted men taking unconscionable risks, began to be replaced by skilled athletes far more interested in winning and staying alive to win again than in displaying their manliness or mad daring.

I think that one of the most difficult parts of racing is being able to control your emotions properly. I've always considered myself an overly eager driver. I could have kicked myself a thousand times, because a thousand times I could have looked good and placed well, but instead I tried to do things I just wasn't capable of doing. I'm well over it now. Before, if I couldn't reach something, I'd jump off the bridge after it, but now, I'll go just so far. Just the fact that I'm able to look at racing patiently and rationally and control what I have pleases the hell out of me.
—Mario Andretti

This is not to say that drivers today lack any of the will to win that their forerunners had, only that a certain professionalism became part of motor racing as the sport's particular nature and the particular skills needed to perform well in it became better defined over the years.

There was a time when the drivers barely deigned to speak to their mechanics. Now, the mechanics—and the team managers, the technicians, the experts, the designers, and the sponsors—share with the driver in the victory.

Motor racing is the sum of its parts— the car first of all, the drivers, the team, the process involved in getting car, driver, and track together, and of course the race itself. Those parts are what this book is out to define.

Whatever is said in these pages, however, may not be true next year. Racing is an immensely fluid sport. Its governing bodies are a tangle of Byzantine bureaucracies whose decisions about which drivers and cars may race against each other change almost yearly and for the most venal as well as the most just reasons. Tracks spring up; others, old and decrepit, are phased out. Drivers realign themselves for more money and a better chance at the checkered flag. Or they retire. Or they are killed.

That the possibility of death or terrible injury is a part of the sport—the most evident part to the general public perhaps—is undeniable. As such, this book will have something to say about the specific dangers of modern racing cars and their safety features, which at least make death less likely. And it will try to discover a little of why a man would take the chances that a race driver takes. Still, the whole answer remains a mystery; it would be presumptuous to state categorically why racers take terrible risks almost daily. All that can really be said is that men have always sought out danger and challenge and that motor racing is the modern arena where they continue to.

1
SUPER MODEL Ts:
The Machines

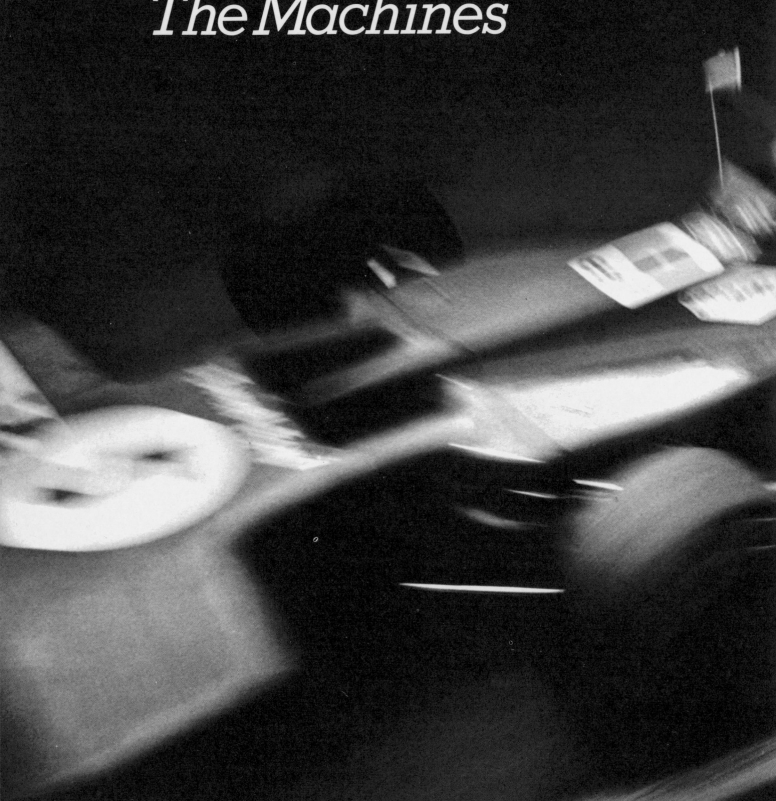

Motor racing is a meshing of man and machine. In no other sport does the equipment have equal stature with the man who uses it. In racing though the drivers are the stars, the machinery is the true focus—just ask the men who design and build it.

These men are among the best, most ingenious engineers in the world, and the cars that they create compare in quality with missiles or jet fighters. More than one racing designer has had a background in aerospace technology. What starts on the designer's drawing board as an abstraction, a figment of aerodynamic notions, arrives at a race track months later a working race car of metal and fiberglass, powered by a highly tuned, very powerful engine.

Because of the rules that govern certain types of racing, the components of many cars are basically stock parts. In some racing, in fact, the cars' chassis and body designs are nearly identical to those of the cars that appear on the showroom floor, although in speed and handling the racing car has little resemblance to its street counterpart. The real jewels of the racing world, though, are the cars that are conceived, designed, and tested to do nothing but race. These are the prototypes, the "formula" cars. Specially built bodies, engines, and accessory systems make them the ultimate in automotive machinery.

These cars—the Ford GT-40s, the Alfa Romeos, the factory teams', the Ferraris, the Porsches, for example—are factory teams. They all come from large production, commercial organizations with a great deal of money behind

Jackie Stewart in his Tyrrell Formula I car comes through Hunze Rug during the 1971 Dutch Grand Prix at Zandvoort.

them. But in England, certainly more than anywhere else, there exists a number of small constructors who have a lot of very good ideas and who are able to make a few very good cars—not many, for the simple reason that they're more or less hand-built. They're more or less worked on by the designers as they go along. Lola comes from one of these concerns.

The engineer behind Lola is Eric Broadley, who's almost typically English, I suppose. He's quiet, a little bit shy, retiring. He doesn't push himself. He's a very good engineer. He's very nice to talk to. He doesn't do any commercial pushing either to further the interest of the factory or of the car. Whether this is a good or bad thing, I don't know.—Vic Elford

Whether the engineer is working on his own in a tiny establishment or for a huge automotive concern, he begins his work with a chassis, around which the whole car will be built. One of the basic problems is to make a chassis that will be very light but at the same time very strong. Different engineers approach the problem differently, but basically the alternatives are "space-frame" or "monocoque." The complex differences between the two can only be hinted at here; though the pros and cons could fill a book, it would be unreadable by anyone but an engineer.

A stripped space-frame chassis looks more like a plumber's nightmare than part of a car. Masses of crisscrossing tubes support one another like bones of an aluminum skeleton. The system of tubes is designed to give the needed strength and support when the engine and other mechanical apparatus is bolted, wired, and welded in

place. Not one strut more than is structurally necessary will be used, the stress on every member is precisely calculated, and if possible, some members perform more than one function. In the Porsche 917, some of the shielded arc-welded tubes in the nose of the chassis even served as return lines from the front oil cooler to the engine.

The monocoque chassis is quite different and, many would say, superior. It has become increasingly popular over the past few years and now is the rule rather than the exception in Grand Prix and Can-Am racing. The monocoque chassis is constructed from various gauges of aluminum sheeting, riveted together to form an inner and an outer panel. The chassis is referred to as the tub, and the driver sits in it just as he might sit in a bathtub. The monocoque tub is usually reinforced in several places to give the chassis added stiffness. These reinforcements are known as bulkheads and are often aided in stiffening the chassis by small tanks for gasoline, which are fitted between the two sides of the tub.

One of the main differences between the two types of chassis is the way the engine is built in. In a space-frame chassis such as the one in the Porsche 917, there's no structural stress placed on the engine; it's simply bolted into the chassis. But in the monocoque chassis, the engine is used as a stressed and integral part of the whole chassis. In other words, the actual monocoque tub forms the front part of the chassis, ending directly behind the driver's head, and the engine is used as the rear half.

Engineers talk endlessly about the advantages and disadvantages of both types of chassis; they even tried to combine the two, as in the Ferrari 312B, in which the monocoque was actually a reinforced space frame and *didn't* use the engine as a stressed member. The men who drive them are, of course, grateful to the engineers for thinking up ingenious ways to make the car light and speedy, but they have another concern as well—how safe is the chassis?

I think that you can say that motor racing has become both safer and more dangerous than it has ever been. For example, the tracks we race on are certainly safer than they have been, with guard rails and safety crews, but at the same time, the cars have gotten smaller, lighter, and faster—more frail and fragile. If you have an accident in a car with a tubular chassis or space frame, it gives you virtually no protection at all. A monocoque frame is far sturdier and a much safer car if you have an accident.—V.E.

So, tubular or monocoque, sturdy or

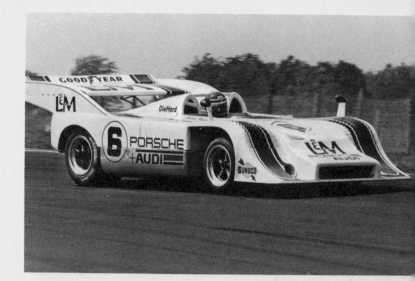

flimsy, heavy or light, a car is a chassis and an engine to power it. The whole thing is then suspended in mid-air from its four corners—the wheels and tires. Once, the wheels rotated simply on the ends of axles, like wagon wheels. Now, a complex combination of wishbones, springs, radius arms, and shock absorbers joins the chassis to the wheels. This mechanism is known in racing as the suspension geometry. The basic theories behind this geometry are universally known among designers, but each man exhibits his creativity when putting these theories into practice. Like an experienced art dealer identifying a painting by a great master, a knowledgeable designer is able to look at a new suspension unit and attribute it to a specific man, based on the man's past designs.

If the engine of the car is its muscle, the suspension geometry is its nervous system. A flaw in the spring settings or tie-rod adjustments is reflected directly in the handling of the car. When a car is built, the suspension is bolted together as the designer's blueprints specify, but the actual fine tuning and adjustments can only be made in trial-and-error testing under racing conditions. In these on-track tests, usually referred to as "chassis tuning" or "sorting out the engine," different spring settings and "sway" bars are tried out with other suspension changes until the proper combination is found.

Suspension failure is one of the major causes of accidents, and although extreme care is taken to crack-test all the metal used in the construction of the rods, hubs, and wishbones, there's always a chance of breakage. A small suspension part can crack unnoticeably under the stress of hard cornering. Later, the sudden collapse of that part can throw the car completely out of control. An experienced driver is usually able to cope with engine, transmission, or brake failure, but when the suspension comes adrift, the process is so quick and violent that control of the car is often impossible.

A car has to stop as quickly and smoothly as it goes. So somehow, powerful brakes must be nestled into the overall design of the chassis and suspension. In oval racing brakes are used sparingly; the good driver can vary the acceleration to make the series of smooth left-hand turns. It's in road racing that brakes are put to fullest use. Sweeping down the last hill at the end of the three-and-a-half-mile Mulsanne straight at Le Mans, the driver of the big Porsche or Ferrari must rely on his four disc brakes to snatch him down from 200-plus miles per hour to 50 or 60 so that he can negotiate the 90-degree turn rushing toward him.

Disc brakes, of course. And on all four wheels. The huge, gleaming discs spin in conjunction with the wheels. The brake pedal is pressed, and two pads on four brakes grab the discs in a viselike grip, instantly generating scorching heat as the car decelerates rapidly. One of the big problems with disc brakes is their inability to function properly under these conditions. Sustained high temperature causes brake fade; it can also cause premature cracking of the discs. To keep the brakes cool enough so that they can be applied time and again in a race, they are cooled by elaborate duct systems, which funnel air

Martini 908 in the countryside at the Targa Florio, 1971.

Clockwise from bottom: *Interior of a Trans-Am Javelin; Peter Revson's Can-Am Lola wrecked and strapped to its transporter after an accident; detail of Revson's Lola.*

Jackie Oliver in the Universal Oil Products
(UOP) Shadow, Watkins Glen Can-Am, 1972.

Clockwise from right: A rear view of the Chaparral 2J, the unusual "sucker" car, shows a snowmobile engine perched atop the regular Chevy powerplant to drive its two fans; George Eaton of Canada navigates one of Road Atlanta's turns; the 2J takes a downhill right-hander during the 1970 Road Atlanta Can-Am; one of car owner Jim Hall's mechanics adjusts the fans before a test session.

Above: *A cluster of velocity stacks sprout from Peter Revson's Lola 222 Can-Am car—longer ones for high end torque, shorter ones for low end torque* Top: *Nanni Galli in the March 721 at Monaco.* Right: *The Carl Haas/L&M Can-Am Lola in the paddock at Road Atlanta.*

through outside body-scoops, through flexible tubing, and directly onto the red-hot surface of the disc.

Sometimes, even that's not enough. The Lotus 72 Formula I car required additional attention when it was standing still. When the car arrived back at the pits after a hard practice session, two specially designed fans had to be immediately put in place over the hot discs. Otherwise, the heat from the discs would have melted the grease in the nearby bearings. Formula I cars like the Lotus usually have little problem with brake cooling, since the discs are exposed to a direct flow of air over their open wheels, but on the Lotus 72, the discs had been moved to the opposite end of the axle, or inboard. This move caused the discs to overheat, but it also reduced the amount of unsprung weight on the car. Most engineers believe that the more weight supported by the suspension and springs of a car, the better. Therefore, Colin Chapman, Lotus's designer, had moved the entire brake assembly—the disc, caliper, and pads—from the inside of the wheel, where it was unsprung weight, to a position closer to the center of the car, where it was supported by the springs of the car.

Now we have a chassis, suspended from the four wheels, with brakes built in to make it stop. Next, is the problem of fuel storage. A huge amount of gas is required to keep an enormously powerful engine running at close to top speed for any length of time. Where is it put?

In order to complete one of today's Grand Prix or Can-Am races, (they average two hours) a car must carry from 50 to 80 gallons

Italian Nino Vaccarella drives an Alfa Romeo Type 33 at the 1,000 kilometers of the Nürburgring, 1971.

17

of fuel. The trend has been toward storing the gasoline in bulging rubber bladders, fitted inside the space-frame or monocoque chassis. For Grand Prix racing, in which any extra space on either side of the driver is used by body panels, fuel is also stored in small bladders, that are strapped either over the driver's legs or beneath his seat.

You fully realize the terrifying dangers of racing only when you first see a driver slip into his seat. He is literally surrounded by fuel. Many drivers can tell grisly stories of accidents in which they have flipped over and, though unhurt, couldn't crawl from under their

cars. Trapped beneath bent metal and fiberglass, a driver suddenly smells, hears, and then sees gas dripping from a ruptured tank. Inches behind his head is a red-hot engine and on all four sides, the scalding brake discs. A tiny spark could set off everything. Many great drivers have no doubt seen it happen and never lived to tell about it.

Another thing that has improved considerably is the equipment we wear. We have fireproof underwear, socks, gloves, hoods, masks, shoes, and suits, along with much improved helmets. But the real trouble in an accident where there is fire

Opposite: *A privately entered, short-tailed version of the Porsche 917 with the two rear fins that were added to the car in 1971 to give it additional stability.* Top: *The Ferrari 512 that David Piper entered and David Weir (USA) and Chris Craft (England) drove to a fourth-place finish at Le Mans in 1971.* Bottom: *Rolf Stommelen (Germany) guides his Type 33 Alfa Romeo through the hairpin at Sebring, 1972.*

is suffocation. A driver knocked out or trapped in a car that has caught fire can suffocate within thirty or forty seconds. The fireproof clothes we wear give about a minute's protection and perhaps thirty seconds of partial protection. But by that time you have probably died from suffocation. I think that any driver with any sense realizes the dangers of fire and racing in general, and nobody goes around saying, "It can't happen to me." I think that everyone is aware of the fact that it can. The only thing to do is to take every possible precaution that we can in equipping the car with seat belts and roll bars and hope for the best.

Jo Siffert's death at Brands Hatch was a per-

fect example of a driver being trapped in a car. I don't think that he was badly hurt from the physical impact of his car hitting the banking, but he was trapped in the fire and suffocated.—V.E.

Gregg Young, a young American driver, came rushing into a hairpin turn on the old Sebring race course during the 1971 12-hour race and suddenly found himself headed toward the dirt retaining bank on the other side of the corner. His Ferrari 512M leaped the bank, flipped in mid-air, and landed upside down on the other side. Because of the construction of the doors on his Ferrari, Young, who was unhurt, couldn't open them. Corner workers rushed to him, and bodily lifted his car into the air. Young scrambled out. A fraction of a second later, the car erupted into flames.

Another miraculous escape was made by Belgian driver Jacky Ickx during the 1970 Spanish Grand Prix. On the first lap of the race, England's Jackie Oliver collided with Ickx in the second corner. The fuel bags on Ickx's Ferrari, filled to the brim for the start of the race, split open and burst into orange flames. Oliver was out of his car in a flash, but Ickx did not appear from the raging holocaust. Finally, after struggling for what seemed like ages, the young Belgian leaped from his car, sprinted across the track, and fell to the ground, his fuel-soaked driving suit ablaze. A policeman quickly dropped near him and beat the flames out. Although not seriously hurt, Ickx still bears the scars on his neck and hands.

All that fuel is supposed to go to the engine, of course. The problem of fuel transfer has used up a lot of drawing-board and testing time, and the malfunctioning of a fuel pump or a valve has felled many a car.

There are some ingenious solutions. For instance, the tremendous acceleration and braking capability of today's cars can be used to transfer the fuel from the bulging main tanks to smaller receptacles, from which it can be pumped more easily to the engine. When the car accelerates, gravity forces fuel through a one-way flapper valve at the rear of the main tank into a "surge tank." Then when the brakes go on, the valve is forced shut by the pressure of fuel in the surge tank rushing toward the front of the car. This operation is

Left: *The Chris Craft–David Weir 512 comes through the Mulsanne corner at Le Mans.* Above: *Switzerland's Jo Siffert in his 908 Gulf Porsche at the 1,000-kilometer race at the Nürburgring, 1971. This car was designed specifically for the Nürburgring and the Targa Florio.*

repeated time and again throughout a race, keeping a constant amount of fuel in the smaller tank. Thus, there's no danger of the fuel pump sucking in air as the fuel level goes down and gas sloshes around in the main tank.

The McLaren team attempted to tackle the difference in handling that occurs when fuel is used up. In the McLaren M19 Formula I car, which was driven for the entire 1971 season by New Zealand's Denis Hulme, a radical new "rising-rate" suspension system was incorporated. As the fuel load lightened during the race, the suspension geometry automatically compensated for the change in weight and kept the car at a constant height in relation to the road. Although some problems were encountered when this system was first employed, most of them were cured as the season progressed. However, the advantage of such a system never seemed to enhance the car's overall performance.

With vast amounts of fuel creating an ever-present danger of fire, all of today's cars are required to carry some sort of fire-extinguisher system. All cars have at least one and

Opposite: *Helmut Marko (Austria) comes off the banking in the Alfa Romeo Type 33 that he drove during the 1972 manufacturers' championship season.* Top: *Niki Lauda (Austria) in his March Formula I car at the U.S. Grand Prix at Watkins Glen, 1972.* Right: *Derek Bell in the Gulf/Mirage sports car that was developed during the 1972 season of long-distance racing.*

23

Top: *The instrument cluster of the Lotus Formula I turbine engine car that was raced on and off in 1971.* Middle: *Rear view of a Formula I car with radiators and suspension in close proximity.* Bottom: *Swede Savage in the All-American Racers Barracuda that he drove for Dan Gurney during the 1970 season.* Below: *Reine Wisell (Sweden) in the Lotus 72 Formula I car, followed by Dave Walker in the Lotus turbine at Zandvoort, 1971.*

often as many as three extinguishers. By pulling or pushing a button, which is usually prominently displayed on the dashboard, a driver can activate the entire system. Some extinguishers are triggered by the mere presence of heat near a sensor. There have been a number of instances when a red-faced driver pulled into the pits sitting in a sea of foam and confessed to his crew that during a hurried gear change or steering manuever, he accidentally triggered his system. But all drivers are glad to have them aboard. The only problem is that the extinguishers are really able to cope only with small cockpit or engine fires. They have proven hopelessly inadequate in combatting major blazes.

The danger of fire will probably always exist in racing because—and now we come to the heart of the matter—the racing engine is an internal combustion engine. The engine mixes gasoline, a highly flammable fuel, with air under high compression, burns the mixture to move the pistons up and down and thus make the wheels roll. In principal, therefore, a racing engine isn't really different from the engine of a Model T. The differences are all refinements. Far more perfect compression, for one thing, is achieved through tolerances Henry Ford never dreamed of—new metals and new ways of forcing fuel and air into the chambers where they are burnt.

It's interesting to note that the top speeds of the cars racing for the manufacturers' championship today are not vastly different from the top speeds of cars in the twenties. (Of course, due to much different suspensions, wheels, and so on, overall speeds are much greater.) It may be that there's an inherent limit to how fast an internal combustion engine can propel a car. If there is, designers have year by year been creeping closer to it—year by year making small improvements on the original idea. This year's racing engine stands as a triumph, a monument, the last word in ingenious precision engineering—until next year.

Some of these super Model Ts are basically stock engines with radical modifications that are designed to draw forth the last bit of power from them. Others are specially forged and cast from the smallest bolt to the block itself. Matra cast the crankcase of its 12-cylinder Formula I engine from an advanced aluminum alloy used in spacecraft. Engins Matra, the firm that builds the Matra power plants, pursues racing as a sideline; its regular business is missile and space-vehicle construction.

As is true in most other facets of auto racing, rules play an important part in engine construction. The rules tell the designers and builders just how much engineering genius they can use in construction. Around these rules they must fashion their plans and theories to extract as much horsepower as possible from a given engine. Their thinking goes something like this: For something to turn fast, it must be light and must generate as little friction as possible. So, although the basic parts found in any engine today are also found in racing engines, there will be more of them in the racing engine, they'll be lighter, they'll turn faster with less friction, and therefore, they'll produce more horsepower.

An ordinary car has one or, at the most,

Clockwise from right: George Follmer in the Porsche 917 Turbo car, which he took over from Mark Donohue when Mark was injured in a testing accident in the car at Road Atlanta. George went on to win the series in the car; Jackie Oliver (England) in the Universal Oil Products (UOP) Shadow car during the 1972 Can-Am at Watkins Glen; the Martini Porsche long-tailed 917 that was driven by Vic Elford and Gerrard Larrousse at Le Mans, 1971.

Opposite: *The Penske/Sunoco/L&M turbocharged Porsche, Mark Donohue at the wheel.* Top: *Denny Hulme (New Zealand) drives the 1972 McLaren "sports car" in a Can-Am race.* Bottom: *François Cevert (France) in a McLaren—similar to Hulme's but a year older—which he drove in the 1972 Can-Am.*

two camshafts. A racing engine is apt to have as many as four, and they will operate four valves rather than two, the number in most street cars. Why four valves? To get more air and fuel to the inside of the engine where the piston can compress the mixture into as small a space as possible. And in order to compress it as quickly as possible, the racing piston is apt to be made of a metal that is stronger yet lighter than the material used in the ordinary car.

With four camshafts operating four valves, the racing engine is capable of consuming a lot of fuel. Engineers have discovered that left unmodified the engine is lazy—it doesn't use as much fuel and air as it can. Therefore, where rules permit, blowers ram air down the engine's throat, and then complex smaller pumps inject fuel toward the cylinder head. Turbochargers, as the pumps that cram the air into the engine are called, are an innovation

in road racing. One of the characteristics of these turbocharged engines is a "lag" between the time a driver steps on the accelerator and the time the engine responds. And as you might guess, there's another lag, this one a little more disconcerting; when the accelerator is released, for a scary moment the car maintains full speed. Finding a solution to this lag had been a problem for road racers until the Turbo Can-Am Porsche was developed in 1972.

As a safety feature, there's a pressure-relief valve on a turbocharged engine, which allows the rammed-in air to be, in effect, "thrown up" when more is pumped in than the engine can take. This valve, the "wastegate," can often be heard bellowing in protest when the mechanics attempt to extract more power than possible from their engines.

Though turbocharged engines aren't al-

lowed in Grand Prix racing, a somewhat similar effect to theirs was created toward the middle of the 1971 season. Air boxes, fitted over the velocity stacks, funneled air directly down the throats of the engines.

A recent innovation in racing machinery is the turbine engine—in principle more like a jet engine than an internal combustion engine. Different enough to be outlawed at that temple of the car, Indianapolis, the turbine engine is still legal in Grand Prix racing.

In 1971, Colin Chapman, the man responsible for the original design of the Lotus turbine cars that appeared at Indy, produced a road racing version of the car, powered by a Pratt & Whitney engine. However, because of the power lag, the car never proved quite competitive. It did have one advantage over cars with a conventional engine. When it came

to running in the wet, the smooth power curve produced by the turbine allowed the car to accelerate from a corner better than the other cars, which suffered from excessive wheel spin. The car was quite strange to listen to. It would appear and disappear with little more than a whoosh from its single exhaust outlet, and the pits sounded like an airport when the driver arrived and shut the engine down with a jetlike whine.

The fierce beauty of a racing engine is accentuated by the other mechanical apparatus that help the basic unit produce the power. Air enters engines through velocity stacks, which are arranged in endless designs. Bolted to the intake manifolds, these stacks line up in perfect military order or sprout upward like clumps of metal trees. Some are topped by massive fiberglass caps or air boxes with one or two large scoops pointed defiantly into

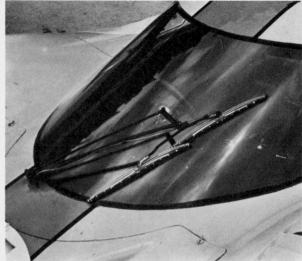

Top: *Windshield wiper of the Porsche 917.* Above: *Charlie Kemp (USA) in a Lola Can-Am car he drove in 1972.*
Left: *Mario Andretti (USA) in his Formula I Ferrari followed by Wilson Fittipaldi (Brazil) in his Brabham at the U.S. Grand Prix, Watkins Glen, 1972.*

Below: *Four double-throated Weber carburetors. These carburetors have been largely replaced by the system of fuel injection.* Opposite top: *One of the long-tailed 917 Gulf Porsches raced at Le Mans in 1971.* Opposite middle: *The powerful lights used for racing at Le Mans on the Martini 917.* Opposite bottom: *Rear hub, brake caliper, disc, and suspension tie rods.*

the airstream. Most velocity stacks stick straight up or at a slight angle to the center of the engine, but some, because of the placement of the cylinders, are nestled lower on the sides of the engine. Masses of wires and tubes crisscross around the top of the engine, carrying fuel and electricity, the spark and the to-be-sparked, separated until they meet in the combustion chamber.

As the fuel, air, and electricity rush through their respective tubes and wires, the camshafts are opening and shutting the intake and exhaust valves with split-second accuracy. The intake and exhaust ports where the fuel-and-air mixture is funneled to the combustion chamber have been cut, tapered, and flow-tested until they are aerodynamically perfect. Smooth, well-polished intake and exhaust ports guarantee extra horsepower. The more mixture sucked in, exploded and blown out, the more power an engine will produce.

Some engines employ dual ignition (two spark plugs per cylinder) to boost power. As if timing one explosion to coincide with the proper valve closing and piston stroke were not difficult enough, dual-ignition engines are often set up so that the two plugs fire in a staggered order—first one, then the other a fraction of a second later.

While these explosive meetings of mixture and spark are taking place, oil and water are rushing through the engine, cooling and lubricating. For racing, in which the explosions are larger, take place more often, and create more friction within the engine than in ordinary cars, these multi-finned, strategically located radiators and coolers are of utmost importance. When oil or water temperatures rise

suddenly during a race, a driver can cure the problem in some cases with a quick trip to the pits. A small piece of paper or other debris from the track may have lodged in the fins of the radiators, causing temperatures to rise quickly.

The exhaust system, which emits the screams, drones, and whines of the engine, has a special twisted beauty all its own. A poorly designed system can rob an engine of horsepower, and the steel twists, turns, and baffles that appear at the rear of the car all have engineering principles behind them. Six pipes snake out from the exhaust manifolds, join into three, pass close to the transmission, and merge again, into one pipe. This pipe in turn is threaded carefully through the suspension and finally pokes out the rear of the car. From the tips of these pipes, comes the engine's beautiful, terrifying, ear-splitting cries. Each make of engine produces its own, highly individual cry. The French Matra engine is responsible for one of the most bloodcurdling

screams in the racing world. At full cry it can clear the wax from anyone's ears.

At the 1971 24 Hours of Le Mans, the sole Matra entry was piloted by Frenchman J. P. Beltoise and New Zealand's Chris Amon. The car lasted well into the early morning before finally expiring. Eating dinner at the small restaurant halfway down the Mulsanne straight, you could hear the distinctive scream of the Matra as it flew out of the Tertre Rouge corner. As it approached the restaurant, which is no more than four feet from the edge of the track, the high-pitched exhaust resonated around the walls. The blue monster shot by in the night, and the whole building seemed to shake. As the car disappeared toward the town of Mulsanne, over two miles away, the scream changed to a whine and finally to a distant moan as Beltoise or Amon decelerated for the 90-degree turn at the end of the straight. Each shift of gears changed the tune as the transmission spoke to the engine.

The transmission, which transfers the horsepower from the engine to the wide wheels, is a maze of gears, bearings, and shafts. With an engine going at 10,000 revolutions per minute (r.p.m.), every piece within a gearbox must mesh perfectly on each gear change. The shift pattern of a Grand Prix or specially built sports car is tiny. Compared to the average car's "throw" (the distance the lever travels when changing gears) of about six inches, the race car's is minute—an inch or two. The shift nob or lever can change from second gear to third with a short jerk or quick flick of the wrist.

The mid-engine design of all specially built race cars not only results in better weight

distribution but also places the transmission in a position where gear-ratio changes and transmission repair are relatively easy operations. The back plate of the transmission, where the gears are housed, can be removed without detaching the entire box from the engine. So when a driver finds that he can use 200 or 300 more r.p.m. when coming out of a specific corner, the mechanics can slip out one third gear from the box and put another in between practice sessions.

Many racing transmissions have their own complete oil systems. Street gearboxes and some smaller racing transmissions have gear oil pumped into them, oil that is cooled as the gears turn and the oil sloshes around, but the real racing transmission generates enough

heat to warrant a separate pump and radiator to cool the gear oil.

After the power of the engine has been transmitted to the gearbox and altered according to the driver's needs by several carefully adjusted forward gears, it exits down the half shafts, or axles, onto the wheels.

The rear wheels used on todays race cars are wide, and they will probably grow wider. The average automobile uses 5-inch wheels. The 1971 Formula I Ferrari used 13-inch front wheels and 15-inch rears. Around each wheel is a squat, fat, bulging tire that is a big part of the superb road-holding capability of the car. Non-mechanical parts of the race car, those fat tires contribute more to the success or failure of the rest of the machine than almost

Opposite: *A rear view of the three-liter Matra driven by Jean-Pierre Beltoise and Chris Amon at Le Mans in 1971.* Above: *The McLaren Formula I car shod in rain tires before the wet Dutch Grand Prix at Zandvoort in 1971.* Left: *The steering wheel and dashboard of the Ferrari 312 Formula I car.*

anything else. Tires, like suspension systems, can cause a car to handle well or poorly. And when they go, they usually go suddenly.

Most of the time when you are driving, you are driving purely on instinct and experience. I think that the brain is like some sort of a computer that stores up what to do in certain situations, particularly in emergencies. A couple of times, I've had incidents where my arms and legs have acted before I've even considered moving them. I had a particular incident that I remember at Spa two years ago. I was coming up a hill in the 917, and we had been having trouble with the tires coming off the rims. One place that you do not want tires coming off their rims is Spa. I was coming up the hill, having done three laps without

any trouble and was flat out on a right-hand curve at around one-hundred eighty miles an hour. The next thing I knew, instead of looking up the road, I was facing the barrier on the right-hand side, my arms were under my knees somewhere, and my feet were jumping up and down on the brake and the throttle as the car slid sideways. The left rear tire had come off the rim completely, and the car was just out of control. My reactions to this were absolutely automatic. There was no question of having to think. If you have to think what to do, it is usually too late.—Brian Redman

Tires come in different shapes—wide, wider, and wider yet; high profile, low profile, in between. They have different tread patterns, and they are constructed from different mix-

Top: *The front of the March Formula I car that raced in 1971 with its nose removed.* Bottom: *Spring, shock, and brake fluid reservoir of the same car.* Opposite top: *The front suspension geometry of the first March Formula I car that raced in 1970.* Opposite bottom: *Air ducts for the front brakes of the 1971 Ferrari 312 Formula I car.*

tures and compounds of rubber. In a practice session, a driver may slip in and out of the pits for tire changes as often as a woman shopping for a dress enters a dressing room. Some tires are good in the dry, some, good in the wet. Others can cope with a little of each. Road-racing tires have to have a greater diversity than their oval-track counterparts; a drop of rain sends the stockers and other oval-track cars scurrying for cover, so they have no need for wet-weather rubber, but rain tires are an essential part of every road-racing team's equipment.

The cockpit of Formula I and other specially built sports cars bears little resem-

blance to the driver's seat of street cars. The most obvious difference is in driver position. In sports cars and even more so in formula cars, the driver reclines in his seat, his legs fully extended as though he were sitting in a particularly restricting chaise lounge. Because rules pertaining to sports cars usually require that there be either a passenger seat or some such area, the sports car cockpit is a bit more roomy than a formula car's, but because all formula cars are open, one doesn't experience the enclosed feeling of covered sports cars.

In long-distance racing—at Daytona, Sebring, or Le Mans—the driver's comfort

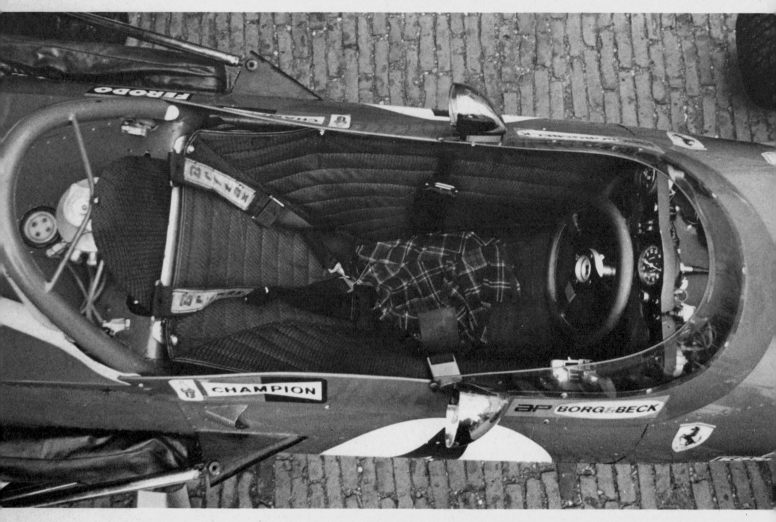

can directly affect his performance. Both the Porsche 917 and the Ferrari 512S (later 512M), which were raced in the 1970 and 1971 manufacturers' championship series, were closed. The men who drove them found the Porsche to be the more comfortable of the two. In a 6-, 12- or 24-hour race, a driver spends a great deal of time behind the wheel. Constant gear changes, hard braking, and high-speed cornering would throw a driver about unmercifully in a conventional seat. The seat of the Ferrari 512 consisted of a metal shell, covered with fire-resistant padding. At two in the morning of a 24-hour race, some Ferrari driv-

ers would be squirming between corners, trying to find a comfortable position in their seats. Meanwhile, Porsche supplied its drivers with form-fitting seats, custom-made for each man. While waiting for his car to pit, a Porsche driver could be seen holding a fiberglass shell covered in foam rubber. The car would pit, one driver would hop out, taking his seat with him, and the new driver would slip his seat into place. Then he would slide behind the wheel.

Some taller drivers require additional alterations in the cockpit before they can be comfortable. For the 1970 24-hour race at Daytona, the Ferrari 512S driven by Dan Gurney and

Chuck Parsons sprouted a bubble on its roof between practice sessions to accommodate Gurney's unusual height. Englishman Michael Parkes needed the same kind of head room in his Ferrari 312P coupe the same year.

All around the inside of the cockpit is an elaborate harness, bolted to the frame of the car. It is designed to keep the driver inside the car in case of an accident.

Of course, the seat belts have improved, and now with six straps to hold you in the seat, you're not going to be thrown out of the car or be dragged upside down under it. You're going to be totally tied into it. If the car turns upside down and slides along the road upside down, you won't even touch the road.

I remember one accident in particular where seat belts saved my life. I was driving a Formula I McLaren at the Nürburgring, and on the first lap of the race, I came up along side Mario Andretti. Just as I did, one of his wheels came off. There was nowhere for me to go, so I hit it. My car went out of control, shot off the road, and flipped upside down. I remember seeing things spinning underneath me and branches hitting me in the face, and then all of a sudden, everything stopped and was very still. When I pulled myself together, I realized that I was lying underneath the car, completely trapped. I could only see out a little corner of the cockpit. Well, to my surprise, there was one of the course workers, standing about twenty yards from my car with a fire extinguisher. He wasn't coming closer or moving away —just standing there. He must have thought that whoever was in the wreck must surely be dead and was waiting for the car to catch fire so he could put it out. About this time I heard the electrics on the dashboard crackling, smelled gasoline, and then felt it dripping on me. At this point I really began to panic. I tried to reach the switches on the dash and at the same time yelled at the idiot who was standing with the fire extinguisher, waiting for my car to erupt into flames.

By now Mario·had arrived on the scene after getting out of his car safely. He ran up and with a few marshals turned the car over and freed me. I found that the arm I thought I had been flipping switches with was actually twisted backward and lying outside of the car, so obviously, I was in great shock. But if I had not been wearing the seat belts, I would have been killed for sure.—V.E.

The instruments that Vic thought he was turning off give the visual printout of the car's internal state. The main difference in specially built race car instrument panels is that there is no speedometer—no gauge that tells you how many miles per hour you're going. Instead there is the tachometer. This instrument tells you how many revolutions per minute the engine is making and is more informative about what is happening to the car.

The instrumentation of a sports car is similar to a formula car's but spread out a bit more because of the available space. The main

40

Clockwise from opposite top: *A drilled disc (to better dissipate heat) and its caliper; a hammer and knock-off bar; a removed engine lying idle during practice; the shift lever and gate of the Ferrari 512.*

Below: *A group of Formula B cars with their wings on struts. After breakage resulted in several serious accidents, changed rules required that the wings be moved lower to the body. Opposite top: Ford engine with air box in place. Opposite bottom: Ford engine without air box.*

instrument is the tachometer. Some have red lines at 6,000 r.p.m., some at 7,900, 8,500, 10,500, or even 11,000. Other gauges measure oil and water temperature, fuel pressure, and oil pressure. Finally there is the prominently displayed fire-extinguisher button.

Once in driving position, a driver finds the gear-shift lever simply by dropping his arm to a comfortable position at his side. The small, thick steering wheel is positioned at the most comfortable distance, and the brake, clutch, and accelerator pedals are at the tips of the feet.

Many people talk about feel. A great deal of it I suppose is through your hands, but a lot of it is in other parts of the body—feet for example. People talk about driving by the seats of their pants. Well it's not only the seat of your pants that's in contact with the modern racing car but your entire body. You are almost lying in the car. Most of your body is in contact with the car. As such, it's subject to the information that the car conveys about whether it is reaching its limits or not.—V.E.

For endurance racing, in which teams of two and even three drivers drive the same car, the physical nature of the drivers must be considered when teams are made up. The pedals, steering wheel, and seat arrangements have to fit each driver. However, in formula racing and certain types of sports car races in which the driver is expected to run the entire race without stepping from the car, the machine can be literally tailored to one man's shape and driving technique. So when sports-

Formula I cars in the U.S. Grand Prix at Watkins Glen, 1972: Left: *François Cevert (France) in a Tyrrell;* top: *Graham Hill (England) in a Brabham;* opposite: *Chris Amon (New Zealand) in a Matra.*

writers refer to "Andretti's car" or "Ickx's car," they mean not only that Andretti or Ickx happens to be driving it at the time but that he is the only one who can comfortably fit in it.

One of the pet peeves of drivers, particularly during summer months, is ventilation. On a hot day, the cockpit temperature of a Can-Am car can reach 120 degrees. On several occasions drivers have been forced to withdraw in the middle of a race because

of heat exhaustion. Peter Revson, the 1971 Can-Am champ, had a Rube Goldberg-type cooling system rigged up in the cockpit of his M8F McLaren. With the flick of a switch, ice water shot down his back from a small hose. Some drivers have ducting systems that blow cooling outside air on them when the cars reach high speeds. Others hook a small plastic tube to a thermos and suck a cold drink while the race is going on. But mostly, they just bear

44

it, well or badly. Comfort, after all, isn't what the designers of these cars are mainly concerned with. The "endurance" in endurance racing applies to the drivers as much as to the cars. Though some minimal comfort is important to a driver's performance, these are men who can bear an inordinate amount of punishment.

Depending on the type of car—sports, formula, or production—the bodywork that covers the chassis and all the innards varies. The production car has its built-in limitations. The general design of the coach work as well as the rules limit what the racing team is permitted to change. In most cases the teams that race production cars just learn to live with the body, perhaps adding a fin or scoop here or there.

But the formula car and sports car have bodies that function as more than just a cov-

ering for the rest of the car. The high speeds and light weights of these cars make the design of their bodies crucial to their handling and aerodynamics. The overall design of the body of the car should permit the air to flow smoothly over it. The less drag that a car has, the faster it will go. And today, the air flowing over and around a car is also put to work. There are fins, flaps, wings, scoops, vents, spoilers, and air dams to keep the car steady at high speeds. The wing in particular has grown in importance lately. It first showed up on the backs of Jim Hall's Chaparrals in the mid-sixties, thrust high in the airstream on two struts. It wasn't long before other teams were adopting the same principle—downward force on the surface of the wing to give the car adhesion in high-speed corners.

Within a year or two, everyone was flying around the track with these strange protrusions sprouting from the rear of the car. By taking the area of the surface of the wing, figuring its angle in the airstream, and then computing the speed of the car, the actual amount of downward thrust on the suspension could be computed.

The immediate result of this new aerodynamic aid was decreased lap times. Cars

Left: *Denis Hulme in a McLaren*. Above: *Dave Walker in a Lotus Formula I, both at Watkins Glen, 1972.*

were sailing through corners as they had never done before. At one point in the development of the wing on the Chaparrals, the driver was able to work a foot pedal that changed the angle of the wing for corners as well as straights.

With the start of the 1970 season, problems started to appear. The overall surface of the wings was becoming too large, and the struts and guy wires holding them were not sufficiently strong to keep them from buckling. Both Graham Hill and Jochen Rindt had wings collapse with disastrous results during the Spanish Grand Prix that year. First, Hill's wing

buckled as he was cresting the rise of an extremely fast section of the course in Barcelona. His car flew out of control and bounced along the guard rail, finally coming to a halt far down the track. A few laps later, Rindt, driving a car identical to Hill's, also had his wing give out, sending him flipping wildly into the air and along the same guard rail where Hill's car had just come to rest. Luckily, neither driver was injured badly. In fact Hill helped to pull Rindt from his mangled car. Shortly after this incident, the height at which a wing could be placed in relation to the body of the car was restricted.

As testing progressed on the wings and on the rest of the body of the cars in general, it was discovered that air dams, small fins on the outer edges of the wings and along the body of the car, kept the air from spilling over the sides, thus creating more effective downward force. Small adjustments on the wings could be translated into more r.p.m. and better lap times.

In 1972, Mark Donohue and Denny Hulme had two monstrous accidents that could be attributed directly to the wing. While testing the new turbocharged Porsche 917 at Road Atlanta, Donohue was involved in a terrifying accident. The rear body section of the car, with it's tremendous wing, tore completely off the car and sent the rest of the car, with Donohue in it, spinning and somersaulting down the long back straight. A somewhat similar accident befell Hulme. Following closely behind George Follmer's Porsche during the race, Hulme pulled out of the slipstream to pass and suddenly found that the change of air currents was lifting his whole car nose-first into the air. The car only had to lift a bit before the wind caught it completely and sent it flipping into the Georgia clay. The same thing happened to Jackie Oliver while driving the TI-22 Can-Am car at St. Jovite. Amazingly enough, each time the drivers escaped without injury.

Definitely one of the most unusual cars to appear on the racing scene in the last few years was developed by Jim Hall with the help of General Motors. Instead of using the natural downward force of wind at high speeds to create additional adhesion, Hall used two powerful fans to suck the car to the road. In addition to the regular motor, which drove the wheels, a second power plant, in this case a snowmobile engine, was mounted in the engine compartment to drive the fans. General Electric supplied sheets of a special plastic material called "Lexan," which were hung around the sides of the car and actually slid along on the surface of the road. In effect, the rear of the car was completely enclosed. First, the regular engine was started, then the smaller fan engine, and the car was off around the track, sucking its way around corners.

At the end of the first season on the Can-Am circuit, the car was outlawed. It seems that the rules state that any part of the car that is used to make a car aerodynamically more proficient cannot be a movable part. After the season was over, it was decided by the powers that be that the fans on the car were breaking this rule.

Also spotted around a car's body are intake ducts, usually of the NASA variety that are found on many airplanes. These ducts are designed to catch the cooling air that is rushing over the body of the car and channel it down through radiators or into other scoops and ducts that lead to the brakes.

Like the cars themselves, the bodies are frail, manufactured from lightweight fiberglass and plastics. Most of the teams come to the track with at least one complete spare set of body panels and sometimes more, depending on the track and the length of the race.

Obviously there is a difference in driving different cars. For example, in sports car racing or long-distance racing, there was a major change between 1971 and 1972. At the start of the 1972

World driving champion Graham Hill of England in his Lotus 72 during the U.S. Grand Prix at Watkins Glen, 1971.

Above: George Follmer in the 1,000-horsepower turbocharged 917 Can-Am Porsche. When Mark Donohue was injured, Follmer took over the driving duties and went on to win the championship. Left: Clay Regazzoni in the original Ferrari 312 prototype that devastated the opposition during the 1972 world manufacturers' championship series. Opposite top: Mark Donohue in the Penske/Sunoco Javelin Trans-Am car. Opposite bottom: Vic Elford in Jim Hall's Chaparral Camaro, St. Jovite, Canada.

Top: Winning *Porsche
917* at *Le Mans,
1970.* Right: *The cockpit of the
Ferrari 312 driven by Jacky Ickx,
Mario Andretti, Ignazio Giunti, and
Clay Regazzoni in 1970.* Opposite
top: *Swede Savage in Dan Gurney's
Plymouth Barracuda Trans-Am car,
St. Jovite.* Opposite bottom: *Piers
Courage in an Alfa Romeo at Le Mans.*

Helmut Marko in the Martini & Rossi Porsche 908 during the 1,000 kilometers of the Nürburgring, 1971.

Clockwise from above: *Peter Westbury in the BRM P160, Watkins Glen, 1971; a large Southern crowd watches Vic Elford crest a rise in the Chaparral 2J at the first Road Atlanta Can-Am, 1971; the factory-backed John Wyer Gulf Porsche 917 that dominated long-distance racing in 1970–71 seen here at the old airport circuit at Sebring during the 1970 12-hour race.*

Clay Regazzoni in a Ferrari Formula I, Watkins Glen, 1972.

season, the restriction on engine size was changed from five liters to three liters.

The three-liter cars really don't have enough power to slip and slide all over the road, so you have to more or less keep them on rails. There just wasn't enough power to waste, as there was in the five-liter cars. They had a great deal more power and an enormous amount of torque in the mid-range of the power curve. This meant that the driver had to be better in some respects because there was really too much power to put it all on the road. The driver had to be very good about feeding all the power carefully to the road and not just simply spinning his wheels all over the place. With the three-liter cars, once you got into the corner, you could simply put your foot flat on the floor because they just didn't have enough power to require any finesse—V.E.

Among drivers there are the specialists and the all-arounders. The one pattern among drivers seems to be first to specialize in one type of racing or car, then to diversify as more and more experience is acquired, and finally, again to curtail one's activity to a specific type of racing and car. Such was the case of Jo Bonnier, who was killed at Le Mans in 1972 on the brink of retirement.

Ah, there's so much you can say about Jo. He was a real gentleman of motor racing. He had been racing for a long, long time in all branches of the sport—in sports car racing, in Grand Prix racing. He won the German Grand Prix a few years ago. And he had tremendous interest in the sport in general—in making sure that the sport of motor racing continued and got better all the time. He used to take a great deal of criticism from everybody—press, drivers, public, and organizers alike—for his work or the work of the GPDA, the Grand Prix Drivers' Association, particularly in relation to safety. In fact, it wasn't usually Jo who was making the decisions. The ideas taken by the GPDA usually came from other sources, and Jo as president was the one who had the job of telling everybody what decisions had been made or what extra safety precautions were required for tracks. So he took the brunt of the criticism.

He was one of the few people, I think, who had continued to totally enjoy actually driving a racing car. Despite the fact that he was by then one of the oldest drivers around, he was still competitive in the sports cars that he chose to drive. When he was no longer competitive in the Grand Prix car, he seemed to look around for the next step down the ladder, if you like, where he could be competitive. He found this in sports car racing, where you don't necessarily need to be the fastest by the tenths of a second that a Grand Prix driver is in order to win.

He raced also all through the European series in two-liter championship racing for sports cars,

where he was perfectly competitive. He was quite capable of winning a race against any of the younger drivers. He never changed. He was very quiet. He was always a nice person—very shy, but he was nice to get on with. I don't think I ever saw Jo really angry about anything.—V.E.

Who are they, then, the men who drive these monsters of engineering perfection? And why do they do it?

Left: *Jean-Pierre Beltoise (France) in a BRM Formula I at Watkins Glen, 1972.* Below: *Matra Formula I engine.* Bottom: *Rear wings and rain tires on a pair of Matras.*

2
"WE ARE ALL AFRAID..."
The Men

**Y**ou've got to want to win. You see the desire in drivers in many different ways. You find drivers who are always trying to convince themselves that they are winners. They strut around, talking big. You find a driver who, off the track, is extremely quiet and shy, preferring to avoid the company of other drivers. You would never consider him a good racing driver. But once he gets into a car, a red mist appears in front of his eyes, and away he goes. Whatever the case, you have to be able to convince yourself, whether publicly or privately, that you're capable of winning any motor race you enter. If you didn't think that you had some chance, you wouldn't race.—Brian Redman

You have to want to win, but as they say in logic, it's a necessary condition, not a sufficient condition. Undoubtedly, there are hundreds of young men—and some not so young—who are well equipped with a desire to win, yet they lack the physical and mental attributes to supplement the desire.

It must be understood that race drivers are athletes, very good ones. The physical requirements of the sport are very exacting, more exacting, in terms of the actual physical skills required to even begin to be competitive, than in many sports. A driver needs strength, though not the brute strength required of a football linebacker or of a shotputter, stamina, and most of all instantaneous reflexes. He needs reaction times near the top of human limit, reaction times that *get better* when the man is under extreme stress.

I think that as the physical and mental requirements on a person are increased, the num-

Mario Andretti in the Ferrari 312 at Monaco, 1971.

Top: *Vic Elford (England).* Middle: *Clay Regazzoni (Switzerland).* Bottom: *Gijs van Lennep (Holland).* Opposite top: *David Hobbs (England).* Opposite bottom: *Peter Schetty (Switzerland).*

ber of people who are able to perform well under these conditions decreases. In other words, the faster a car goes, the smaller the number of people who are able to drive it. But also, the sheer costs involved in racing limits the number of people who are able to compete in the upper levels of racing. Since there are only about twenty-five to thirty places available in Formula I, the places are very hard to get, and the series is therefore very competitive with a great deal of pressure involved.—Jacky Ickx

It's extremely hard for the average person to imagine what it is like to drive a racing car at the speed and skill that is required, mainly because it is something that the majority of people haven't done. The basic road car relates very little to a race car. Although the principles behind the race car and road car are related, a race car has been refined and tuned to such an extent that the resemblance is distant. It is hard to describe the difference in feeling between a standard production car and one that has been modified for racing but harder still to describe the feeling one has behind the wheel of a real race car.

Luigi Chinetti, Jr., son of Ferrari's American distributor, has competed over the past few years in a number of endurance races in production cars and in prototypes—cars specially designed and built to be raced. Until 1970, he had never driven a prototype. His first encounter with such a car was during the Sebring 12-hour race of that year.

Our cars and those of the factory Ferrari team were all lined up outside the garage at the track in Sebring. It was the day before official practice, and the mechanics had set up a short triangular course for us on some of the roads on the abandoned airfield. We were just supposed to run around the course a few times to make sure the cars were basically all right. The car I was to drive with Tony Adamowicz was a 312P, the closed three-liter coupe which was a distant relative to the winning 1972 open version.

I got into the car, which was a feat in itself, and settled down into the seat. At once I wondered what I was doing there. To my right was the small knob of a gear-shift lever, no bigger than three inches. In front was a wheel so small I could almost touch my thumbs across the diameter. The windshield was low, the roof of the cockpit was two inches above my head, the seat was uncomfortable, and I was unpleasantly cramped. And I was supposed to drive this thing and race at speeds up to one-eighty. Again I asked myself what I was doing there.—Luigi Chinetti, Jr.

An old racing chestnut says that if an ordinary man were given a road car and told that he was absolutely safe, that he could drive along a five-mile stretch of road as fast as he could without danger of an accident, he would still drive at nowhere near the car's limits. The man who would drive really quickly would be a top racing driver or a man who had the potential to become one. Top racing drivers must surely be born with some of their skills.

As far as I know, that test has never been actually staged. But psychologists have made studies of racing drivers, with interesting results.

A group in America was doing psychological tests on racing drivers. The psychologists tested

a lot of people, starting with strict amateurs, and progressing up the ladder. They discovered that the higher grade of racing drivers have the ability to do things that nobody else or very few people have the ability to do, that is, to get better under stress.

For example, they gave us routine tests on paper or made us fit pegs in holes. If the tests are given at a reasonable speed and without any stress there was little or no difference between a driver, a football player, and a business executive. But as the stress and outside diversions become greater, drivers become better at their job while others just go to pot.—Vic Elford

There is a new branch of technology—or perhaps a new bud on an old branch—that is developing the "cyborg," a cybernetic organism. Basically, a cyborg is a combination of man and machine—for instance, a mechanical hand and arm that can lift huge weights and is attached to and operated by a man, who gives it the same instructions he would his own arm and hand. A computer translates the mind's directions to the arm's muscles into directions for the machine.

A race driver in his car is, in a certain sense, a cyborg. The relationship between him and his car is almost symbiotic, especially in today's cars, which are so light and so responsive. The great difference, of course, is that there is no intervening computer to translate a driver's wish to turn left, take evasive action, or brake late, into instructions to the car. The driver must do all the translating himself, instantaneously, while the car is traveling at very high speeds. So rather than the car becoming a part of the driver, it must be the

Opposite: *Ronnie Peterson (Sweden) in March Formula I car.* Top: *Vic Elford.* Above: *Ignazio Giunti.*

59

other way around—the driver must become the car. His senses must be its senses.

I think that the prime sense is the sense of touch. Sound doesn't come into it except that your ears are accustomed to the correct sounds, and if an incorrect one creeps in, then, despite helmet and ear plugs, you can still recognize the sound that shouldn't be there. In terms of sight, you tend to be concentrating only on the instruments in front of you that you need to look at now and again, the road in front of you, and the mirror.

But the prime sense is feel. Driving a car to its limit is a bit like trying to walk on eggs, I suppose. You know if you make a mistake the results might be disastrous. Or it's like walking a tightrope. You've got to know when you're about to fall off. You've got to keep balanced however far you might lean over. This is probably why a lot of people have accidents during their early days of racing. They haven't developed the sensitivity to know when they are coming to their own or the car's limits. Once you've gotten through that period, learned about the point at which a car is unrecoverable, and can drive it to that point and no further, then you become a good driver.—V.E.

That is the basic skill, and if race driving were like chess, with precisely defined rules and limits, it would be all that was required. But it's not. The random variables thrown at a driver under high-speed conditions are many, ranging from the condition of the track, to the weather, to how safe he feels his car is, to the competition he's getting from other cars and drivers. The *gestalt* that the driver is able to perceive while traveling at high speed and negotiating turns surprises even himself at times.

It's funny, really, when you're racing, even at high speeds, I don't really feel that I'm going terribly fast. You can see people standing by the side of the track. Quite often, I can recognize journalists when I'm going maybe one-hundred and thirty or forty miles an hour. And you take it all in, and maybe you're thinking about something else besides racing. You don't just concentrate on the narrow strip of road in front of you; you take a general view of everything you can see as far ahead as possible, which is very important. For example, at Spa, during the thousand kilometer race there in 1972 when I was driving a Ferrari, I had this kind of awareness. I had been taking one particular corner just about flat out in fifth gear, which made it an extremely fast curve. On one circuit of the course, I noticed something strange happening in the crowds along the side of the road as well as ahead of me.—B.R.

The fast curve came at the bottom of a hill. Brian was following another Ferrari, which shot over the hill at top speed and flew down into the curve and promptly spun out. Brian, though, had already begun to brake, because he had seen that people in the crowd were beginning to put up umbrellas. Though he had felt or seen no rain himself, he realized that farther down the track, it must be raining and that the fifth-gear corner just might be wet and not negotiable at top speed. He was right.

As it was, I did a bit of on-and-off-the-brakes and twisting-of-the-wheel, but I managed to slip through and stay on the road. I'm sure that if I'd come over the hill and around the curve under full steam, I would have been in trouble.—B.R.

Racing is not simply a test of the man and his car. It's a competition. The tests that Elford said showed drivers getting better under stress also showed that they were highly competitive, a fact one hardly needs a psychologist to define. The hierarchies of racing are as strict as any aristocracy's and just as capricious. Every man knows how he is regarded, whom he is better than, whom he has beaten, and who has beaten him. He feels, perhaps, that he has not been shown to best advantage yet, but that doesn't really count. The only thing that really counts is how well he can be shown to have done—in lap times and position.

I think that I am a rather careful driver. I know my limits, and I know the limits of the car. If I don't know them, I try not to go to what <u>may</u> be the limit. But I can go much faster if I have a direct fight with someone or if there is a chance of winning. I have to see it directly and be involved in a direct match with someone else to drive at or near my limit.—Helmut Marko

It's for this reason that the racing world and racing drivers in particular are so mesmerized by numbers. A group of drivers talking can sometimes sound like a class in the new math; fractions of seconds matched with revolutions per minute, lap times from years ago remembered and argued over. Numbers don't lie. They tell you exactly how well you did and thus how good a man you are. All drivers know about the accidents of fate that can get a man into the winner's circle or keep him out of it, for that matter. But they have a certain faith that the record books will eventually tell the whole story. Certainly they will tell more of a driver's life than the trophies he has accumulated.

I suppose I've changed a lot really since I started racing. At first I wanted people to recognize me as a successful driver, and the trophies were

Left: *Mark Donohue (USA) at the wheel of a Ferrari 512.*
Above: *Peter Revson (USA).*

important to me. Back in the very beginning, in 1959 and 1960, they were very important. You know, little egg cups and things like that were placed in prominent positions, and once, I think when I won some money and no prize, I even bought a cup and had it engraved, a terrible thing to do.

Now the trophies are not important to me. In fact, we were talking of having them melted down a few weeks ago and making a table with just a few badges on it. They're all shut away, apart from a good one or two, and whether I would want to look at them later in life, I don't honestly know. I don't think so. They don't mean much. If you want to remember your racing life, you can do it without trophies.—B.R.

Probably one of the first and hardest things that a driver must do at the start of his career is to come to terms with the dangers of motor racing and the effects it will have on him.

I think the process of meeting the danger involved in driving a racing car is a large part of the pleasure of driving a racing car. I'm sure that this is the pleasure that mountaineers get and that probably bull fighters get. In any sport like that which involves a certain amount of inherent danger, I think that the pleasure comes after the confrontation. During the race and before it, you are concentrating too hard to enjoy it, but afterward, you get a tremendous feeling of well-being and relaxation. Everything looks better. The sky is bluer, the grass is greener because you've been on the edge of, I won't say death, but of considerable danger. You've done something that's the absolute limit of your ability, physically and mentally, and you've done it successfully. You don't have to win the race to be very satisfied with the race. You may finish third or fourth, but if you've done your very best and you've performed up to your expectations, then it's an extremely satisfying sport.—B.R.

The danger of the sport is something that's forever in your mind because a driver can be hurt or killed so easily. Naturally, it's something that bothers you a bit. You have to contend more or less with a law of averages, but you have to accept it. It's just like driving down the highway in the morning. You see a lot of accidents, but you know damn well that you're not going to walk to work. Just like on the highway, in racing you have to say, "Well it won't happen to me. I'll be a little more careful." That highway driver, after passing the accident, slows down by ten miles per hour, but twenty minutes later, he forgets about it and is right back at his original speed.

Of course, you're going to be exposed to danger, but that's really what makes the sport so unique. You're defying something. You're doing something that makes most people shiver just thinking about it. You feel like you have something that others don't have. Now and then a driver's death really hits you below the belt and knocks you for a loop, but then you figure that's the price you have to pay, and you keep doing it because you love it. There can be sacrifices involved, and it's not a bed of roses all the time by any means, but there is nothing else I would rather be doing, and there's no other way I could get as much satisfaction out of life. You won't hear any Monday morning blues from me about having to go testing, or flying to another race. I love my work, and how many people can truthfully say that? That's what life is all about as far as I'm concerned—doing what you love most. Sometimes it doesn't come cheap, but sometimes you get away with it.—Mario Andretti

One of the reasons a racing car is so dangerous is that a compromise must be

made between safety and weight. For example, although a roll bar is designed to protect a driver from being crushed in the event of an accident, the weight of a really protective bar would cause the car to be uncompetitive. The unbelievable energy and destructive power that is unleashed in an accident cannot be fully dealt with. The roll bar could prevent one thing or another in an accident, but in some cases it could end up hurting rather than helping. Therefore, when a driver steps into a racing car, no matter how safe it is alleged to be, he undoubtedly realizes that he is reducing his chances of dying a natural death.

I don't think that drivers are generally worried that they will make a mistake and crash. They worry about something breaking on the car, which happens quite frequently. I think in my own experiences I have had probably ten or twelve breakages in the last four or five years. They haven't resulted in accidents, but they very easily could have.—B.R.

A driver cannot plead ignorance in his evaluation of the dangers of motor racing, for history has shown that drivers are killed and killed with regularity in the sport. Perhaps the rate has dropped over the years because of the evolution of safety in cars, but as each new year of racing begins, there is generally someone absent in the ranks of top drivers.

After each race that Porsche won during the years 1969–71, the company had a very nice poster designed and printed. It listed the winner's speed and times and, since Porsche was mainly involved in endurance racing, the top five or six finishing cars and their co-drivers. One day Brian Redman looked at a

Opposite: *Jackie Oliver (England).*
Top: *Carlos Reutemann (Argentina).*
Above: *Graham Hill (England).*

65

Left to right: Toine Hezemans (Holland); Herbert Müller (Switzerland); Helmut Marko (Austria) drives Alfa through hairpin at Sebring 12-hour race.

poster of a race that he had won in 1969 and realized that of all the names on the list of top finishers, he was the only driver who hadn't retired or been killed. "It was really a bit sobering," he said.

In spite of the proven fact that accidents resulting in serious injury and death happen to the absolute best, the great majority of drivers continue in the sport.

When you become afraid, when you think that you may have a crash, I think that is the time to stop racing because then you can no longer be competitive. Now I am more afraid that I may make a mistake and because of this lose a race. —J.I.

The danger and death aspects of motor racing are woven into and through the entire racing world, and it is this more than anything else that sets racing apart from other sports.

One might think that the gathering of drivers almost every weekend of the year at race meetings would produce dozens of close relationships among them. However, the majority of drivers seem to discount this.

Nowadays, unfortunately, the competitiveness of racing in general really prevents you from becoming close friends with another driver. You are trying to beat your friend out on the track, and there are people who are trying to get your job. But in spite of all the rivalry, you are basically on friendly terms.—Helmut Marko

It's true that there usually aren't many close relationships in racing, I suppose partly because there is a chance that your friend may be killed suddenly. I've never spoken to anybody about how I feel when a driver is killed. We seem to say "Oh what a shame, what a great bloke," and on you go with the race.

Before I became involved in big time professional racing, if a top driver who I didn't know was killed, I felt "Oh well, a shame, but this is racing." But once I got into it, knew the people

66

well, and in some cases was very close to them—like Jo Siffert, my codriver for two years when we drove for Porsche, and Pedro Rodriguez who was a teammate—it became a different story.

Each time one of these drivers is gobbled up, it hits very hard, very hard indeed. And you think, well, I'm going to stop. It's a waste of time, what we're doing. There are other things in life besides motor racing. Yet just a couple of weeks later, you think, well these people died doing something they enjoyed more than anything else and in which they were better than most people in the world, and they got probably more satisfaction from racing than from any other job. They will always be remembered as being at the peak of their prowess and because of this will be remembered more dearly.—B.R.

I think that Jo's death really affected me more than any other driver's because certainly he was my best friend among drivers and had been for a long time. He was really the only person whose

death made me think, "I'm going to give up racing right now." I had been good friends with Paul Hawkins and Piers Courage, but Jo's death had a bigger impact on me than a lot of others did because my two boys were both very close to him and his wife. I really thought that I was going to give up racing right then, but after a week or two, I was able to get over the initial shock.

I suppose the last death of a driver that really shook people was Jimmy Clark. I think that everyone felt Jimmy was just too good to die, because there was no way that he could make the sort of mistake that would result in a bad accident. He didn't make a mistake. Something happened to his car. But I think everyone was badly hit by his death because he was so good, because nobody thought that anybody that good could possibly die. The rest of us know we've got limitations, even Jackie Stewart. I don't think that anybody has really felt that Stewart is invincible, whereas Clark was one of the very few drivers who was really head and shoulders above everybody else.

I don't think anyone ever felt Jo Siffert was immortal. He was a real fighter who would never accept defeat. He occasionally had accidents, and you were always aware that he really was fighting for everything, so it was always conceivable that an accident could happen.—V.E.

The game of racing is a deadly serious business, and the track is no place to settle petty differences. Drivers are well aware of this, and the cases of intentional jousting on the track are usually few and far between and then confined to production and sedan racing. Here, the consequences of cars touching are generally less harmful than similar comings-together by the more delicate and dangerous road racing machinery. Chances are that the aggressor in any encounter between sports-racing or formula cars will end up as badly off as the fellow he has been trying to knock off the track.

Besides being a sport, and a dangerous one, racing is a job—precarious, difficult, unstable, and totally demanding. Few careers require such dedication and have so little room at the top.

The public mind is hard to change, and there are drivers who resent the public's notion that race drivers are either mindless goons with no thought for life or limb or that they're international playboys living a mad orgy—an "eat-drink-and-be-merry-for-tomorrow-we-die" sort of thing. Neither is true, of course. The life-style of most professional drivers in the top rank is probably comparable to that of a top-flight international salesman with perhaps a little movie star thrown in.

The public concept of a racing driver varies I think from locale to locale. In America the people that I've met seem to think that all racing drivers are rough mechanics and rather dubious characters. I could be wrong on this, I don't know, but this is just the overall feeling I get from people who aren't connected in any way with racing and who don't know anything about it. The same holds true in South Africa. When we went to live in South Africa, we eventually became good friends with our neighbors. But at the beginning they didn't know what to expect. They were horrified when they knew a racing driver was coming to live next door. They thought that there would be hotted-up cars rushing up and down the road all day and grease-covered mechanics crawling out from every bush.

In Europe I think that being a racing driver is thought of as a respectable job. It used to be that the popular impression in Europe was always that racing drivers were wealthy playboys and that it was all parties and booze and women. This was probably so up until fifteen years ago when the pattern of racing changed completely from a wealthy man's plaything to a serious professional business with very large amounts of money at stake. It's not to say that we don't enjoy ourselves now, but we're so busy going from race to race that there's very little time for parties or relaxation.—B.R.

Perhaps three of the seven days in a driver's week are spent at a track, practicing, qualifying, or racing; two are wasted in travel, getting there and back; and the other two are juggled in resting, testing, or endorsing. One weekend in May 1972, Vic Elford's schedule read as follows. *Friday:* Practice at the Nür-

Clockwise from top: *Mark Donohue (USA); Mario Andretti (USA) in the Ferrari 312 sports car; Tim Schenken (Australia).*

burgring in the Eifel Mountains of Germany; *Saturday:* Practice for a Formula 5,000 race at Crystal Palace in England; *Sunday:* Back to Germany for the 1,000-kilometer sports car race; *Monday:* Back to England for the Formula 5,000 race.

As strenuous as it is at times, travel is one of the things that makes the sport appealing. When one closely examines the schedule and agenda of a top road racer, at times it looks like a world tour for a VIP. One would get little argument from the top drivers in motor racing over the contention that the life of a professional road racer is very desirable.

You know through your contact with the sport, you change. At first you are traveling a lot, seeing foreign countries all over the world, meeting very interesting people in racing and outside of it in business, cultural, and political life. And, of course, you learn from them, and after a while you change, naturally, in your character.—H.M.

Another common misunderstanding— perhaps wishful thinking is a more accurate description—concerns how race drivers begin in the sport and get to the top. The image is the same as the one in the old boxing movies—tough promoter sees slum kid beat up thug and says, "I like your style kid. You're pretty good with your dukes. How'd you like to fight for me?" It doesn't happen that way in boxing or in racing. Behind almost every top driver are years of racing in minor classes, driving uncompetitive cars under catch-as-catch-can circumstances, and a very gradual rise.

Jacky Ickx is an exception, such an outstanding exception that he proves how rarely

the rule varies. His rise was, to put it mildly, meteoric.

You know I never had a desire to become a race driver. When I was thirteen, my father, who was a racing journalist, took me to Spa-Francorchamps for the Grand Prix. It was so boring that I asked him never to take me to another one. Just leave me at home where it was quiet. So my father bought me a motorcycle, which I learned to ride, and before long I was entering local trials. It was a Zundapp 50 cc. bike that I rode the first year and on which I did quite well. The next year I became the works driver for the Zundapp factory. For the next two years, I did well in each category as I moved up in the size of the motorcycle. When I was eighteen, the importer of the motorcycle, also the importer for BMW [Bavarian Motor Works], offered me a ride in a car. Then it seemed that there was always someone who would offer me something bigger. Each year I would move into a bigger car—first 700 cc. salons, then 1600 cc. salons, and then a big

Mustang salon, then Formula III, Formula II, and finally Formula I.

I think that my real break came in 1967 when I was doing a season of Formula II. I had won one or two Formula II races, and then there was a combined Formula I and II race at the Nürburgring. Formula I was for the Grand Prix of Germany, and the Formula II cars were just there to fill up the grid since the Nürburgring is so long around one lap. I had set the third fastest time of the Formula II cars and in some cases faster than the Formula I cars, but even so, they started all the Formula II cars behind the Formula I cars. After eight laps I was fourth, behind Jack Brabham's Formula I, and could not get by him because his car was faster than mine on the straight sections of the track. On the last lap, my wheel came off, and I had to stop. But even so, a lot of people had seen me driving and offered a Formula I drive for the next year. But Ferrari was the first to ask me and also offered me the best contract to race for them. This was the first time that I realized there was a financial side to racing. It has always seemed relatively easy.—J.I.

One can imagine no experience more unlike Jacky's than Vic Elford's. After the war racing was just starting in England, and his father took him to a Grand Prix race in Silverstone. From that moment he wanted to be nothing but a racing driver. His family wasn't rich, he had no money, and he had no idea how to begin. He had spent his first years in a car, but not racing.

Clockwise from opposite bottom: Pedro Rodriguez (Mexico); Jackie Stewart (Scotland) in a Tyrrell; Arturo Merzario (Italy); Derek Bell (England).

As it turned out I started by chance. I was at school, one of my friend's parents won a big sweepstakes, and they bought him a car. We

71

started rallying together, with him driving and me navigating. Then after a year, he sold the car, and I joined another man to go rallying. We both wanted to go international, but we couldn't afford it. So we decided we'd do as much as possible until we became good enough to get into a works team, which we ultimately did, and rallied with them for three years.

I had started to drive a little bit, had a car by then, and made no secret of the fact that I reckoned I could drive better than some of the works drivers. So the next thing I knew, I was thrown off the team, which I suppose was quite reasonable since navigators were not meant to be drivers. Being thrown out, I was able to buy an ex-works car from my former employers, BMC [British Motors Corporation]. I drove that for a while and then landed a job as a works driver for DKW of Germany.

In 1966, I switched to Porsche, doing rallies, and then did my first real race with them at the Targa Florio, a course that's suited to a rally driver. From there one thing led to another.—V.E.

In racing one thing does not quite lead to another. Success requires good performance in racing and then the know-how to capitalize on that good performance with those who count —the companies and manufacturers who sponsor racing. Tim Schenken started in Australia, not exactly the center of world motor racing.

Unfortunately, I didn't win the Driver-to-Europe award, which is given to the up-and-coming person who needs financial support to pursue his racing activities on the continent. Some forty-two-year-old won it, which didn't really make a whole lot of sense to me.

In 1966, I came to England, with a mate of mine who used to be a mechanic for me, and I hoped that I could just sort of break into professional motor racing. My goal was to race Formula I. I didn't have any money, so I just went along on the off chance that something might turn up. What turned up was a big nothing. Nobody was going to give a car to someone who had just

72

Opposite: *Nanni Galli (Italy) in a March.* Below left: *David Hobbs (England).* Below right: *Tony Adamowicz (USA).*

arrived from down under, so the only solution was to borrow some money from my father, with which I bought an old Formula III Lotus, did some development work on it, modified it, and raced it in club racing until 1967.

My performances were good enough to land me a race in a Formula Ford. With a little luck and before I knew it, I was driving the second-team Brabham car in Formula I. Then Piers Courage was killed at Zandvoort, and I took his place in the De Tomaso. Well, 1972 was rolling around, and Ferrari was very interested in Ronnie Peterson. But they were interested in him only for long-distance sports car drives, where two drivers were needed. They needed someone to team up with Ronnie. Jacky Ickx and Mario Andretti were not much good for them because they were too short. They needed someone relatively the same size as Ronnie. That was me. I would say that my contract with Ferrari for the sports car drives in 1972 was a combination of luck, being in the right place at the right time, and being the right height.—Tim Schenken

Denis Hulme, Jack Brabham, and Bruce McLaren were three drivers who started their careers on the end of a wrench and then moved behind the wheel, preparing the cars they drove. Jo Siffert's father was the owner of a car agency, and Jo, like Pedro Rodriguez, Jacky Ickx, John Surtees, Mike Hailwood, Jean-Pierre Beltoise, and others, started his career on two wheels and later moved to four.

Most drivers can remember one particular episode in their career that they can say was a turning point. Those persons who were financially unable to buy a car and to gain recognition by driving it probably remember more than others a phone call or a conversation that launched them on their driving career. Most drivers can also remember their first trial by fire, in which they had to show their stuff for a team manager.

Usually the driver in question has come to the attention of a team manager because of his previous performance in lesser races. A phone call may come out of the blue to the driver, asking him to appear at a certain track to test a certain car. In other cases the car to be tested has been set up by a team such as Brabham, Tyrrell, Penske, etc., and generally the number-one team driver has already driven the car at this particular track. Therefore, the team manager has some indication of what a competitive time is.

The selected driver must take the car, with which he is usually unfamiliar, and perform. He drives it around the track in so-so times, or is outrageously bad, or is outrageously good. He knows that he must drive at competitive speeds to be selected as a team driver, but he also knows that if he tries too hard, spins, and damages the car, it may be the last time that he is given a chance by that particular team. The rumors of his performance may spread to other teams, and before long, the word may be out that he is a waste of time.

There's no question about it that being in the right place at the right time has a lot to do with success in racing. I know that one of the most critically important drives I had in my early years as a professional driver was with John Wyer for the nine-hour race in South Africa, where I drove with Jacky Ickx. This was my first big opportunity, and I know that I drove above myself in this race. I pushed beyond my capabilities, nothing went wrong, and we won the race. Because that drive went well, I was offered a contract for the whole year of 1968. If I had had an accident, it could have finished me.

The positions within teams are so hard to get nowadays that one bad race—maybe through no fault of your own—can finish you. Just like that you go from the top of the heap to the bottom. I have seen very competent drivers take the gamble, perhaps drive harder than they were capable of driving at that time, and have an accident. And that was it.

Being there at the right time got me one of the Ferrari factory three-liter sports cars for the 1972 series. Pedro Rodriguez was to have driven a new BRM [British Racing Motors] in the Interserie, the European equivalent to the American Can-Am, but Pedro was killed driving a 512 Ferrari at Nürnberg in the previous race of the series, so BRM offered the car to Sid Taylor. He was supposed to drive a McLaren at Imola. When he switched, I took the car at Imola, where, as it turned out, the conditions were really appalling. It poured rain, but I had a good day. The car felt good, and I won the race. In fact I lapped the entire field.

As it happened, there were some people at the race from Ferrari with a car that was being driven by Clay Regazzoni. They saw what I did and asked if I would be interested in doing one or two races for them the next year when they occasionally would run a third car. I told them that I would, and then two days later, their team manager, Peter Schetty, phoned me and asked if we could meet in London. He said that they were in fact interested in running a permanent third car throughout the year. So I met with Peter the next day at the London airport and signed the contract.—B.R.

The matter of wealth can be a factor in the sport, and no one will question the fact that the easiest way to get into racing is to buy a car and learn to drive it. However a great many drivers have had to break into the sport with their talent alone.

I'd been messing about for a while in the beginning when I got this call one day from a chap named Charles Bridges who had just bought a lightweight E-type Jaguar. He asked if I could be at Oulton Park the next morning at nine o'clock. I presented myself, and there was this beautiful lightweight E-type. It was a very special car with an aluminum body and an aluminum block. The factory had only made about fifteen of them, much rarer than the D-type.

Charles Bridges had a fastest lap of one fifty-five, and the record for the class was one fifty-one. On the fourth lap, I did one forty-nine eight. I stuck my neck out and went faster than I was really capable of driving. Bridges asked if I would like to drive his car, and I, of course, said yes. I think that I entered seventeen races in the car and won sixteen of them. So I was feeling pretty good about racing and had driven just about all the English circuits when a private entrant asked me to drive a GT-40 Ford at Spa in Belgium. I said yes, great, and along we went, since I thought I was well-equipped to drive anywhere at all. After the first day of practice, I nearly wanted to retire from racing and go home.—B.R.

But of course he didn't. It was a major step toward what Brian has become—one of the best sports car drivers in the world. It was no doubt a little scary to take that first step at Spa, a track that is generally acknowledged to be the most inherently dangerous among major European tracks because it can be, *must* be, taken flat out nearly all the way around. If you're not willing to take the chance of going flat out, if you lift your foot when it's not absolutely necessary, you'll fall back. Brian had the nerve and just as important (as we

Top: *Alex Soler-Roig (Spain) and Nanni Galli (Italy)*. Middle: *Mark Donohue (USA)*. Bottom: *Parnelli Jones (USA)*.

75

saw in his story about the rain at Spa), the judgment to keep up. Now he had the car as well. After Brian's several years in motor racing, all the elements had fallen into place for him.

In the case of a driver who has bought his own car—a competitive car—to get started in motor racing, it's sometimes very difficult for him to prove to the rest of the world that he is as serious about the sport as a driver who began with only his talent to support him and who got into the seat of a good car only after a long struggle. But this is the way that Piers Courage and Jochen Rindt started, and surely no one will contend that either was any less a driver for it. There have always been complaints from certain quarters about drivers who get and remain where they are because they have bought their rides. Often the grumbling comes from drivers who have less money and who feel they have more talent. It seems that this will remain one of the facts of life in the sport.

There are very, very few individuals who could maintain themselves in the upper ranks of motor sports on their own finances alone. The costs are astronomical. Even when a driver can buy his way in, he is usually buying only a place in the lower ranks or a shot at a place in the top. If he's good, he'll attract the kind of sponsorship that can pay huge bills. If he's not, he quits or settles for a relatively cheaper position in sedan racing, for example.

Once established, by whatever means, the driver always has a pack of young talent snapping at his heels. At the end of each racing season, rumors fly, drivers negotiate, there is a mad shuffling of contracts and

drives, and deals are made left and right. The very best drivers are paid handsomely for their services, both by the teams they sign with and by individual sponsors whose products they endorse or at least allow themselves to be associated with.

If the money for endorsing a product doesn't go into a driver's pocket, it goes to pay the expenses of the car he drives. Wherever the money goes, there's a lot of it; more and more companies, increasingly remote from the automotive world, have looked to racing and race drivers as an outlet for their advertising dollar. Nor does it seem to bother a cigarette company that a driver whose helmet is blazoned with its name smokes cigars or doesn't smoke at all. Visibility is the name of the game, and racing drivers are highly visible.

An example of a driver who gets a lot out of racing—probably because he puts the most into it—is Jackie Stewart. He is not only one of the most successful drivers but also one of the richest. Now living in Switzerland instead of his native Scotland—for tax reasons as well as the logistics of racing life—Jackie Stewart spent most of the time that he wasn't at the track traveling around the world, promoting the sport and his name. He curtailed his activities in 1972 when he developed an ulcer, possibly the result of constant globe-trotting. He took a few weeks off and then returned to the field for the French Grand Prix, which he won handily.

Less active in racing matters when he's not at the track is Belgian Jacky Ickx. During the 1972 1,000-kilometer race at the Nürburgring, Ickx's codriver, Clay Regazzoni stuffed their Ferrari into the guard rail, dam-

Clockwise from bottom: *Clay Regazzoni clowns with an admirer; Jacky Ickx (Belgium); Reine Wisell (Sweden).*

R. WISELL J. BONNIER
G. LARROUSSE

CHAMPION

FERODO

GOODYEAR

but there are other things. Four days or more out of the week I devote to racing, and the rest of the time I spend elsewhere. I have my house, and I have my business in Belgium, which must be looked after for when I retire.—J.I.

When he made these remarks, Jacky was well shy of 30 years old. But already he was preparing for his retirement.

The average working life of a race driver is, compared with some sports, fairly long. A man can still be racing successfully when he would have been out of swimming for 20 years, out of football for 10. Graham Hill won the 1972 24 Hours of Le Mans at the age of 42. But in racing, unlike some sports—golf or bowling, for instance—your abilities can go suddenly, and you'd better not be racing when they do. Also, many drivers feel they have a certain quota of luck, and when that is used up—whether at age 40 or at 25—it's time to retire.

I am sure that a moment will come when you have a feeling that you have done enough, that your potential for luck has come to an end, because there is a certain amount of luck involved in motor racing. When you almost have an accident and escape without damage, you use some luck. When you have a bad accident and escape with minimal damage you use some luck. Eventually, there is a moment when something in you says "My luck is all used up. Now you have done enough."—J.I.

The decision to retire is usually a tough one. Drivers who retire do so with a good bit of pain and anguish, as do all athletes who finally realize this is the last time they'll be

aging the suspension and putting the car out of the race.

I was in my car, driving back to Belgium before the race was over. I had completely forgotten about the race, and I was only reminded about it when the winners, Ronnie Peterson and Tim Schenken, were announced on the radio. For me, when the race is finished, it's finished. I don't think about it after I have made an analysis. I know where I have to take the good of the race and the bad of the race, and I just dismiss it from my mind.

For me, racing is a very important business,

doing something they have known and loved for so long. Brian Redman retired temporarily at the end of 1970.

I wanted to live a normal life, basically. I felt it was unfair to the family and to the two children that I should have a type of life where I spend at least half my time away from home. Every time you leave home, you don't really know if you're going to be back again. This sort of thing got a little bit on top of me, so I retired from racing, went to live in South Africa and started a job as manager of a Volkswagen agency. As was predictable, as two or three dozen people had told me, I couldn't stand the normal life. It wasn't nine to four, it was eight to seven and Saturday mornings, and I think I saw less of the children. But basically, I couldn't stand the aggravation of business, the constant nattering, not actually dealing dishonestly but dealing—not being entirely straightforward.—B.R.

Brian returned to racing, a classic case of false retirement. It's not as common as among movie stars but hardly uncommon. When he'd decided that racing was really where he wanted to be, he had the problem of getting back into it—getting a good ride and proving to himself that he was still competitive.

It took me about three races to get back into the right frame of mind after I came out of retirement in 1971. It's a bit similar to when you're hurt in a bad accident. There's a very big difference between that and having the biggest accident in the world where you come away unhurt. You think, "Christ, that was a bit nasty. I don't want another one of those soon," but within half an

hour of driving a car again, you are back to normal in terms of your driving capabilities.

But when you've been badly hurt, it takes longer. You don't really want to drive the car hard, and every time the car starts to break away into what would be a normal slide, your heart jumps into your mouth, and you think, "Oh Christ, here we go again."—B.R.

Soon after coming out of retirement, Brian was hired by Porsche to drive in the Targa Florio with his former partner, Jo Siffert. Redman had won the race with Siffert the year before in a Porsche 908-3.

The 908-3 was a car developed by Porsche in 1970, specifically for races like the Targa Florio and the Nürburgring, which are difficult and demanding, with a lot of tight corners and a lot of braking. It was a very light car—very light indeed—and a very nice car to drive.

The Targa Florio is a very special motor race and really the only one of it's type left in the world where you race on public roads. One lap is in the region of forty-four miles, and there are supposed to be something like nine hundred corners per lap. I've never actually counted them, but I have no reason to doubt it.

You have a variety of surfaces. The course winds up through the Sicilian Mountains, and because of its length, it is difficult to police properly. In other words, it is difficult to provide adequate safety arrangements, such as ambulances or first aid areas.

Now in this particular race in 1971, I had practiced in the car, and it was pretty satisfactory. My codriver, Jo Siffert, had had a small accident in the car, and the chassis had been bent a little

Clay Regazzoni peers out from the cockpit of the Ferrari 312 in which he won his first Grand Prix, at Monza, 1970.

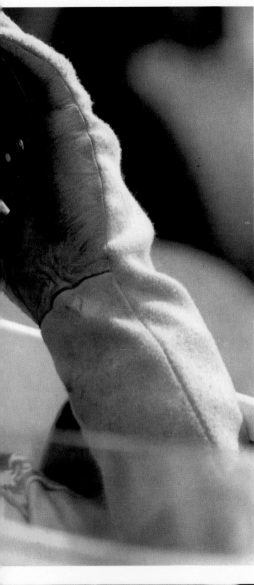

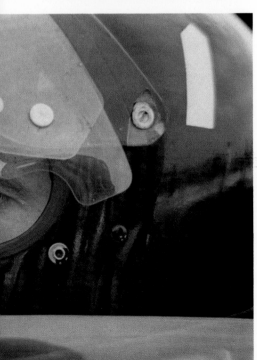

Clockwise from above: *England's Derek Bell; Graham Hill; Piers Courage; Switzerland's Jo Siffert.*

Clockwise from bottom: *Austrian world champion Jochen Rindt; Graham Hill, a man whose face is filled with experience; Italian Arturo Merzario in his country's colors; New Zealand's Chris Amon, a veteran with a great deal of talent and very little luck.*

Clockwise from above:
America's Mario Andretti;
England's Richard Attwood; Jo
Siffert at Monaco, 1971;
English Ferrari driver Mike
Parkes; Jacky Ickx of Belgium.

Above: *American Can-Am veteran Lothar Motschenbacher.*
Top: *Jackie Oliver, English and extremely talented.*
Right: *Italy's Arturo Merzario in a happy mood.*

bit in one place. As it turned out, I never was able to drive the car again before the start of the race.

Normally, Jo Siffert, whom I had driven with for two years in 1969 and 1970, always started first. He was the number-one driver, and I would always drive second. However, for this race, because of some interteam tension, it was decided that I would start the race. That was a little unusual, and the car had a different type of tire on it than the one we had been practicing with.

Not having driven the car in its new state, I was off at the start. Well the handling wasn't very good—at least not as good as it had been in practice. I was in fact having quite a bit of trouble with the car and had completed something in the region of eighteen miles, struggling all the way, when I came to a particular corner which I knew quite well. I don't know all the corners on the Targa Florio as some drivers say they do, but I know the worst ones. This one I did know because one of my friends, Richard Attwood, had crashed there two years previously.

I came down to the corner which was a downhill left-and-right-hander, taken around the eighty to ninety mile-per-hour mark. I turned into the left-hand part, and instantly, everything went wrong. The car shot straight across the road and hit the bank on the other side. The car exploded into flames. The next thing I knew, I was sitting in an inferno. In my mind I knew that I had to get out very quickly. I had my eyes shut tight, and I was holding my breath because I knew that if I didn't get out within that breath, I wasn't going to get out. I know, as do most race drivers, that if you take a breath in a fire, the oxygen is burned out of your lungs, and you will pass out.

As luck would have it, I'd practiced getting in and out of the car about ten or twelve times the

81

Left: *Derek Bell (England)*. Below: *Chris Amon (New Zealand)*. Opposite: *Jo Siffert at the Targa Florio.*

night before with a stop watch in preparation for the pit stops. Instantly, I hit the seat belt and was out. But of course when I had gotten out, I still had problems. My overalls were soaked in petrol, and I was on fire from my ankles up to my waist. I could hear someone screaming, either myself or one of the spectators. I ran to a little hill and rolled down it, beating at the flames as I went. I knew what was happening but didn't really know what to do about it.

Eventually, I got the flames out and stood up just as some spectators came running up with blankets. I went with them to one of their little tents and took off my overalls. By this time my hands and legs and face were very sore, particularly my face. For this race I was using the lighter open helmet rather than the full-face type because the great number of corners would make my neck muscles very tired after a few laps and cause me to lose concentration.

The only part of my body that was not protected by fireproof clothing was an oval circle around my nose and eyes. As a result, this part of my face was quite badly burned. Having taken off my suit, I just sat in the spectator's area and waited for help. It got more and more painful. The spectators were fanning me with shirts and newspapers, but there was no medical treatment available whatsoever. Again, because of the peculiar nature of the circuit, no assistance or help came for something like forty minutes, which seemed like a lifetime. Eventually a helicopter came and had some trouble landing, but they got me back to the pits, where I was laid down for a time to try to get rid of some of the shock before I was taken to a local hospital.

They should have taken me to the hospital in Palermo, but instead took me to a local hospital up in the hills. Nobody from our team knew where I was. The next twelve hours were the worst in

82

my life. I was unable to see because my face had blistered badly and my eyes were completely shut. I was unable to communicate with anyone since I spoke no Italian and they spoke no English. There was a chap in the bed next to me who had been hit by a car in the race, and was dying. His mother was with him, screaming, and he was screaming. I was there for twelve hours before anyone came. It was extremely unpleasant, to say the least.—B.R.

That is the sort of experience that would seem to make a man want to retire from driving. But Brian Redman, who gave up driving to lead a "normal life" and couldn't

stand the strain, who came back and met with one of the most gruesome accidents a driver can have, is still racing. More often than not, what makes a man retire is the mirror image of what made him start. He feels that he's no longer good enough, that he will begin to fall behind, that he cannot be competitive any longer.

I will quit the day when I no longer have the fun I have now—or when I begin to be afraid. We are all afraid—afraid to make a mistake which will cost a race, afraid of doing badly. I am afraid now. But to be really afraid. . . . Then I will quit.—J.I.

83

3
A SMALL ARMY:
The Teams

In 1972, Peter Schetty was 29 and in his second year as Ferrari's team manager. The prize was the 1972 World Championship of Makes, and Ferrari, after a languid effort the year before, had decided to go all out to win it. The drivers they had contracted were among the world's best: Ickx, Andretti, Redman, Regazzoni, Schenken, Peterson. The cars were newly designed and were well-supported with money from Fiat, Ferrari's parent company.

Peter Schetty was in a good position as a team manager since he spoke four languages. He had been a prototype driver himself and had the full confidence of the factory as he set out to win the championship.

Actually, a team manager's job starts at the beginning with the drivers and cars. First, you must have the drivers. Let's suppose you do have them, because at Ferrari we generally sign a contract with a driver for the entire year, and they are more or less at your disposal. Then you must have the cars, which is not really a problem of mine, but of the engineers. They are responsible for having the cars sorted out and ready on time.

Now suppose you have an international championship race. If it is a long-distance race you must decide on the proper combination of drivers. Then you must start the whole organizational operation, which means you must find flights and arrange for rent-a-cars and hotels for the drivers, the mechanics, and anyone else connected with the team.

Transportation of the equipment is another important factor that must be taken into consideration. There must be flights for the cars and equipment and trucks to take the equipment from

Peter Warr, left, team manager, Emerson Fittipaldi, driver, and Colin Chapman, owner and designer.

Below: *Alfa Romeo in the pits at the Nürburgring. Team manager Carlo Chiti, right, talks to driver Nino Vaccarella. Opposite: David Yorke, team manager for many years with John Wyer, chats with the head mechanic of the Gulf Porsche team.*

the airport to the track. Organizers must be dealt with. Letters have to be written to them with an entry, and an agreement must be made over starting money, the amount the team gets merely for appearing and racing at a track. Sometimes, this takes quite a long time. Sometimes, there is an argument between the organizer and the team manager as to just what the team is worth.
—Peter Schetty

Long before all this, Peter negotiated the contracts between the drivers he so casually supposed he had. In most cases the teams and drivers are able to make an arrangement

of some sort without a great deal of fuss. There are few "holdouts" in the racing world and few drivers who demand outrageous fees and astronomical bonuses. There are too many other drivers with talent and ambition, waiting in the wings, ready to sign for half of whatever fee is being offered by the team. To be asked by Ferrari to race in a season the company is out to win is a chance few drivers would refuse. Witness the caliber of the team Ferrari in fact assembled.

If any additional lure was necessary, it may have been the fact that Peter understood drivers because he had once been one. He

was good enough to have been teamed on occasion with Jacky Ickx but not good enough, by his own estimation, to become one of the handful at the top.

You first break into racing, and, if you are lucky, progress up the ladder toward the top. Eventually, you are able to find out what you are capable of doing, and in my case, I found my limit. In order to be really competitive and win, I would have been risking my life. I would have been pushing myself more than I should have. And in racing few drivers actually feel they are risking their lives. In my opinion, if you cannot be one of the best or don't think you can become one of the best, you should stop. Today more than ever in a lap of two-and-a-half minutes, if you are one or two seconds behind the best times, you are out of business.—P.S.

It turned out, though, that Peter had precisely the right combination of talents to be an excellent team manager. Credit must be given to the superbly designed Ferraris and of course to the drivers, but Peter Schetty deserves a large part of the credit for a season in which Ferrari won every race it entered. And the drivers give him that credit.

Ferrari is an Italian team, and as such Peter Schetty, the team manager, was invaluable. By nature Italians are very excitable, but Peter had the ability to keep everyone under control and keep people doing what they should be doing without getting too emotional. Peter seemed to be able to put it all together in 1972 and choose the right drivers and tires and help keep everyone under control. Of course, his ability to speak so many languages fluently was a great asset in his job.

The relationship between Peter and the drivers was almost a father-and-son relationship. We all act like kids at times, running off to the swimming pool or tennis court or golf course. We

ask "daddy" when we have to be someplace.
—Tim Schenken

Daddy's firm hand was required at times on the track as well, and sometimes the drivers bridled a bit at that. Ferrari was out for the Championship of Makes. It made little difference to Ferrari who won a given race, as long as he was in a Ferrari. The title would ultimately go to the car and not to the driver. This meant a strategy of holding off at times, shepherding all three cars through long races so that one of them would last the distance and finish first. There were times when the drivers didn't quite see it that way.

To Jacky and me, the steady-pace and finishing-second stuff was bull. We just gotta go; win or blow—that's all. The manufacturer doesn't look at it that way, but we do. Schetty has a tremendous amount of responsibility because, obviously, he has to call the shots from the manufacturer's end. A bad call on his part could blow the whole thing. I've seen that happen—not with him but with other team managers. It was a real plus—his conducting his job as team manager just properly—not only in dealing with overall strategy but dealing with the men as such. He understood a lot of our problems, and it makes a lot of difference. The man knew what the hell goes on inside a driver's head and what he could and could not get away with. He knew damn well he couldn't hold us to a team strategy per se. Like yesterday—the Ickx–Andretti team won, so today it's the Regazzoni team. Bullshit like that we just wouldn't stand for.

At the 12 Hours of Sebring, we were really shakin' it. Those cars are kind of fragile,

and you're talking about 12 hours. At one time Regazzoni and I were really fighting each other, doing some pretty fancy times. I came in, and Peter said, "You guys are crazy! You're going to blow both cars!" So I said, "Look, I'm leading now, and he's not gonna pass. That's all there is to it. You slow him down and I'll slow down. . . ." Poor guy. I can imagine him going through that all year long. At Watkins Glen we were way out front—there was no competition but ourselves—and if both of us would have blown. . . . I mean that guy was going through nightmares. To us, you know, you blow an engine—boom, to hell with it. But if both our cars had fallen out as far ahead of the competition as we were, it would have been his head on the chopping block.
—Mario Andretti

Of course one reason Peter Schetty could afford to let his boys have a fairly long tether was that he was fairly sure his cars *wouldn't* blow. The cars had been carefully tested at Modena, and when it appeared that they couldn't last 24 hours, Ferrari didn't enter them at Le Mans. For all the other races, Schetty knew his cars would last—they lasted and won. By the time of the running of Le Mans, Ferrari had the championship won.

Peter Schetty's chief competitor in the 1972 manufacturers' championship series was an Alfa Romeo team managed by Carlo Chiti. A man of the old school who had been around, first with Ferrari as an engineer and design expert and then with Alfa Romeo, Chiti was in the unfortunate position of competing against Ferrari, Peter Schetty *and* Fiat money during the 1972 season.

Right: *A scorer and timer wearing his ear protectors at Le Mans.* Bottom: *The interior of a pit with all tools laid out ready for use during the 24-hour race at Le Mans.*

Alfa Romeo's team manager, Carlo Chiti, is really one of the most interesting characters in motor racing. He's an enormous man physically. One of his favorite pastimes is eating and drinking good food and good wine. He's very excitable, and every now and again, it's quite normal to see him clipping a driver on the ear like a teacher slaps a naughty boy in school. With Chiti you always know where you stand. The most characteristic thing about him is that he gets very excited almost to the point of punching you, and then five minutes later he's got his arm around your shoulders, and he's laughing with you. One of the problems at Alfa Romeo recently in the organization of the team is that there is no real hard team manager. In 1972, Chiti did the job of team manager assisted by Marelli and Ceveri, the two other engineers. But in fact all of them were a bit too nice to be team managers. The drivers were frequently allowed to get away with things that a hard-nosed team manager would not have allowed.

For example, some of us were racing at the Nürburgring on Sunday and in England on Monday. I commuted back and forth over the weekend for both practice sessions. Ferrari also had two or three of their drivers involved in races in England. But Schetty said quite simply, "Your first contract or commitment is to Ferrari and you stay here at the Nürburgring until the thousand-kilometer race is finished, and then if you wish, you can go to England." Though I benefited by being able to pop back and forth, from the morale point of view of the team and from the efficiency point of view, it would have been much better if I had been made to stay along with the other Alfa drivers at Nürburgring.—Vic Elford

93

Both Peter Schetty and Carlo Chiti were managing factory, or "works" teams, so the one problem they did not have that most team managers have is arranging for a sufficient flow of money to keep their teams afloat. Though the possibility for team sponsorship is widening to many different industries, it's still not easy to get sponsorship sufficient for a team's needs and loyal enough to see the team through bad times.

Nowadays, most teams would be unable to survive without sponsors. At Ferrari it was a little different because Ferrari is an automobile manufacturer and has ties with Fiat. But in general the sponsor must pay the bulk of the expenses since the prize money and starting money a team receives from the organizer is insufficient. But then the problem of using a sponsor is that one never knows if the sponsor will be supporting you next year.—P.S.

Ken Tyrrell, the British team manager and actually a lumberman by trade, is independent of a factory. Tyrrell has to tend a flock of highly sensitive contracts with Elf, Goodyear, and a dozen others. It often puts one in the position of crawling on one's knees while shaking one's fist and so demands a certain agility.

Racing's eternal triangle is formed by the sponsoring company, the team, and the sponsoring company's ad agency. The company has an idea of what it expects to put into the project financially (which is often not what the team thinks it needs) and the ad agency knows what it expects to gain in advertising. The team is in the business of racing, the ad agency is in the business of promoting the sponsor, and the sponsor is in the business of

selling at an efficient cost–profit ratio. The three goals are not mutually exclusive—if they were, there would be no sponsorship—but they are sometimes in conflict. So men like Ken Tyrrell, Roger Penske, Teddy Mayer, and Frank Williams, to name only a few better-known examples, must keep one eye on the team and one eye on the checkbook.

Factory team or independent team, the difference that a team manager with drive and strong organizational talents can make is obvious. Ferrari had been run into the ground by the Porsche 917s for two seasons and had run only one car, an experimental 312P, the following season, 1971. John Wyer was the Porsche team manager, and the factory backed him with everything he needed. He came equipped with superb managerial skills, an engineer's sense, trained through many seasons, and a hand-picked team of drivers and mechanics. Ferrari put up no such effort.

When the international governing body of motor sports changed the rules for the manufacturers' championship, theoretically to even up the competition, they outlawed the five-liter engines with which Porsche had won so consistently. Working with a three-liter upper limit and with a year of mistakes behind them, Ferrari, with Peter Schetty at the helm, proceeded to take the 1972 manufacturers' season apart. In many cases Ferrari finished one–two and in one case one–two–three. Porsche had retired from racing, and John Wyer was developing his own three-liter car, which remained experimental throughout the season.

When Roger Penske became the manager of factory-backed American Motors Javelins, the team was in bad shape. The pre-

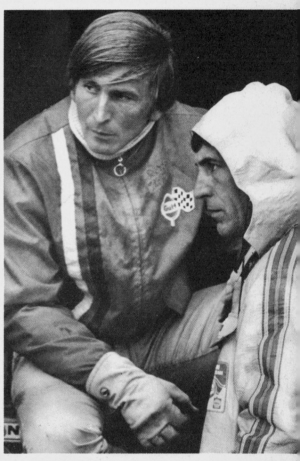

Left: *left to right, Brian Redman, Tim Schenken, Ronnie Peterson, and Clay Regazzoni, part of the 1972 Ferrari long-distance team. Above: Derek Bell, left, and Vic Elford, who drove Porsches for different teams during the 1971 season.*

vious two years, the cars just never seemed to be competitive. In fact they rarely finished. Penske was hired to make the cars win.

Javelin hired not simply a man but an entire team—Penske; Penske's driver, engineer, and alter ego, Mark Donohue, and Penske's engineering and mechanical staff, an organization that functioned like clockwork. By the time the first race of the season was held, the Javelins were already the favorites. The sly fox from Philadelphia had "Penske-ized" the entire effort and was giving both the Chevrolet Camaros and the Ford Mustangs a run for their money.

Besides being a masterful organizer, the team manager has to be a master of personalities. He must know how both drivers and mechanics—and sometimes sponsors—will react in certain situations. A hundred decisions have to be made. Mechanics must be hired, upgraded, fired; so must drivers. If a driver isn't making the grade, he's got to go—

Opposite: *Jacky Ickx and Ferrari engineer Mario Forghieri.*
Above left: *Colin Chapman, the founding father of Lotus.*
Above: *Jackie Oliver climbs into the 917 he drove with Pedro Rodriguez at Le Mans, 1971.*

99

and quickly—so that the team effort isn't dragged down. It's the team manager who has to tell him. He also has to tell a driver to relinquish his car to the number-one driver if number one demolished his own car in practice. That takes a certain amount of tact.

When I was team manager for Ferrari, we employed top drivers, and they know how fast they can go. The driver is behind the wheel, and if he says, "Look, I can't go any faster," or, "The car isn't handling properly," you have to accept that. One of the reasons a man has become a professional racer and drives fast cars is his confidence in his ability to do just that. He must be like "the little engine that could." If a team manager is constantly pestering him to do better, then the driver himself will surely develop doubts about his ability to perform up to his own and the team manager's expectations.—P.S.

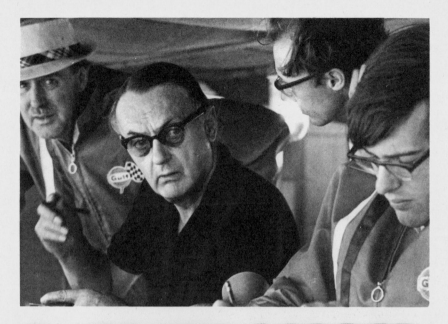

Opposite: *Roger Penske, left, and Mark Donohue seen through the interior of their Ferrari 512.* Top: *John Wyer, middle, a master of long-distance racing.* Bottom: *Helmut Marko in the Martini Porsche 917 that he codrove to victory with Gijs van Lennep in 1971 at Le Mans.*

It would seem unusual, considering the unstable nature of the sport and the pressures on the men, that there are many instances when a rapport develops between a driver and a team manager and keeps them together for years. Roger Penske and Mark Donohue come to mind, as do Ken Tyrrell and Jackie Stewart, Denny Hulme and Teddy Mayer. This almost symbiotic relationship is one reason they're successful. Whereas in most cases the driver–

manager relationship is at best professional and courteous and at worst stormy, unpleasant, and short, the successful ones are warm friendships. They are formed during the days spent together in the pits, on airplanes, at the dinner table.

It was like that between Colin Chapman and Jimmy Clark, but that relationship ended in a grove of trees near the rain-slicked track at Hockenheim during a Formula II race. Frank

101

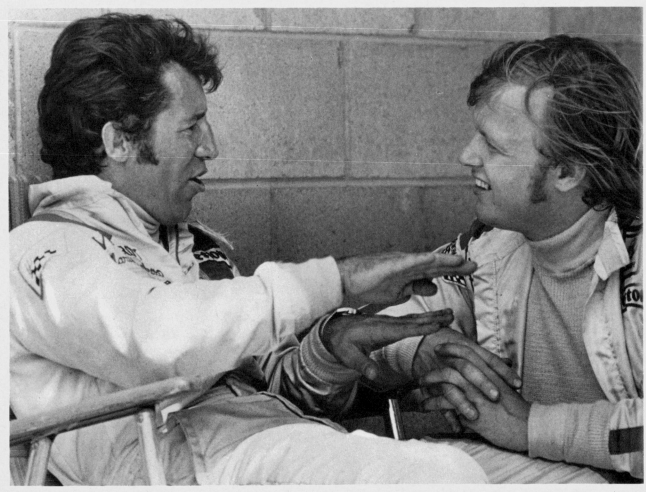

Clockwise from below: *Taking times during practice; Mario Andretti, left, and Ronnie Peterson; Dan Gurney, left, and Pedro Rodriguez.*

Williams and Piers Courage had such a relationship that ended in a fiery wreckage in the sand dunes near the track during the Dutch Grand Prix. And it might have been that way between Colin Chapman and Jochen Rindt had Rindt not gone out of control at the Curva Grande in practice for the Italian Grand Prix.

Whose fault is it? Was the suspension piece that the team manager elected to use too fragile? Did the transmission lock because he decided not to have it rebuilt the night before?

The Italian authorities added to Colin Chapman's misery at Monza following Rindt's death. Chapman had been through this before —a man dies, and someone must be held responsible. In the minds of the authorities, the logical person is the car owner and builder. So in the midst of his anguish, Chapman was forced to flee the country for fear he would be held and charged with a crime for what is an inherent part of motor racing.

Motor racing is a hierarchical sport, though perhaps not as much as in the past.

Below: *Ferrari mechanics pose prior to the six-hour race at Daytona in 1972. Opposite: The Alfa Romeo Type 33 in the hands of Helmut Marko, their rival during the 1972 season.*

At the top of the racing-team hierarchy are the drivers, arranged in a hierarchy of their own, from top to second-rank to lower-rank—an unstated order, perhaps, but one of which all the drivers are intensely aware. Next is the team manager, then the chief engineers, the top mechanics, and finally the lesser mechanics.

The mechanics are the proletariat of the racing class system. A good mechanic on an American racing team can make $250 or $300 a week, which, worked out into an hourly rate, isn't much at all. European pay rates are lower. A racing mechanic has to love what he's doing.

On the team that supports a race car, the mechanic is the man closest to it. It's he who puts the car together, changing it from a mass of metal to something almost alive. He knows every wire, weld, and spring by heart. To a lot of drivers, the car is no more than a car—if it performs well, it's done its job, but if it fails, it has betrayed its master. Perhaps a locked brake has sent it into the guard rail—filthy beast refused to stop. Now it lies at the side of the track, its nose, fashioned with such care, a shattered mess. The driver walks away. The mechanic, though, has just spent weeks working on that one part of the car. Minutes after it left the pits in perfect trim to practice, it returns on the hook of a tow truck, and the mechanic's long job begins again. A mechanic's job isn't nine to five; it's over when the job is done. That may mean working through the night to repair an engine or a transmission so that a car can be on the starting grid the next day when the green flag falls. Overtime is rarely mentioned. If the mechanic

Opposite: *Sweden's Reine Wisell being strapped into his Lotus Formula I car.*
Below: *Rolf Stommelen secured in his Alfa.*

has worked until the minute the flag falls and if the car is off, fixed, and racing, then those long hours have paid off. Of course, no matter what happens, the mechanics are paid, but if all that work goes to waste, it hurts a real craftsman, and most racing mechanics are just that.

Out on the track, the car is running well. The driver is gaining positions; he's third, then second, then first—but then he doesn't come around on the next lap. A few minutes later,

word comes that the car has stopped on the back straight or, worse, has crashed on the back straight. The mechanic thinks about what it was he didn't tighten, or. . . . Then the driver is back in the pits, and he's joking with him because it's not that bad, not as bad as it could have been.

The factory teams of mechanics that flock to the races number up to 16 or 20 men, gaily clad in multi-colored uniforms. As the sport has become more commercial, the staid,

drab colors have disappeared from the mechanics' backs. Now, the pits can look like a tropical aviary.

During the 1971 race at Le Mans, the Porsche Martini team, more a factory team than a truly independent team, was putting up in a garage in a small town near the track. One of the long-tailed 917s had been wheeled into the streets, and its chassis tubes were being welded. The mechanics from Stuttgart were gathered around it as busy as a crowd of German elves when a French farmer came by in an ox-drawn cart with a load of hay. The Porsche was blocking the road, and the German mechanic made it clear that the car wouldn't be moved until the welding job was through. The Frenchman threw up his hands and muttered that he thought the German army had been driven out of France a long time ago, but that possibly he was mistaken.

Maybe that kind of arrogance comes with being the best. A Porsche 917—perhaps that very one—was driven to victory at Le Mans that year by Helmut Marko.

Opposite: *Swede Savage, left, and Peter Revson, teammates at Sebring, 1971.* Right: *Derek Bell, left, and Jo Siffert, teammates for the 1971 season of endurance races.* Below: *Colin Chapman sprints down the edge of the track at Zandvoort after learning that Dave Walker crashed at the end of the straight in the Lotus turbine car.*

Opposite: *Emerson Fittipaldi (Brazil) speaks to a reporter.* Above: *Juan Fangio, former world champion driver, chats with Jo Siffert and an attractive companion.* Left: *Pedro Rodriguez discusses strategy with David Yorke (obscured).*

The character of teams is very different. This obviously has something to do with the nationality of the team that you are driving for. In 1971, I drove for the Martini racing team in Porsche sports cars. With the Germans, I would practice for a while and then head into the pits. All I would do is tell them what was happening or going on with the car, and then they would make the decision as to what to alter.

But the next year I drove for Alfa Romeo, and the Italians were completely different. We would come into the pits and tell them what was happening with the car, and the mechanics would ask you to make the decision about what you would like.—Helmut Marko

Although there can be an occasional rift between driver and mechanic, more often the driver–mechanic relationship is a case of reciprocal admiration. One can see this in the eyes of both parties after a high finish or a victory. The driver may acknowledge the cheers of the crowd, but he also realizes that without the skill of his team of mechanics he

Below: *The start of the 24 Hours of Le Mans, 1971.*

Opposite: *An L&M team mechanic straps Peter Revson into his
Lola prior to the start of the Mid-Ohio Can-Am race, 1970.*

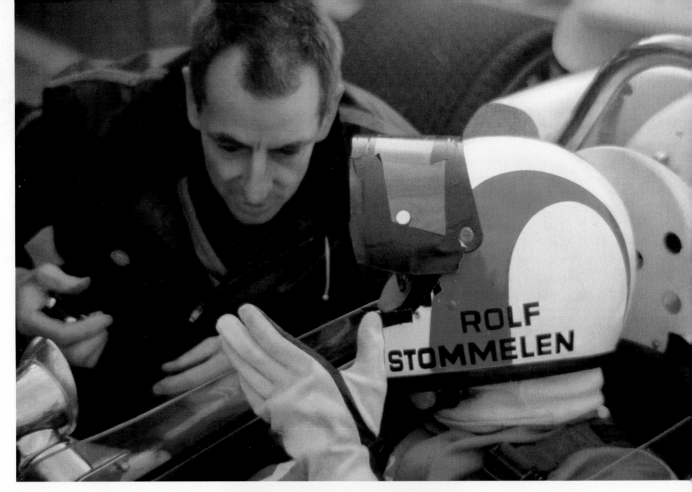

Clockwise from above: *Rolf Stommelen discusses his car's handling with its designer, Ron Tauranac, during practice for the U.S. Grand Prix at Watkins Glen; veteran driver Jack Brabham, left, gestures as he speaks with Rolf Stommelen; Swedish driver Reine Wisell talks with a Lotus team member while special fans cool his inboard disc brakes; Graham Hill listens as a technician talks with him about various tire compounds.*

Clockwise from opposite top: *Car designer Colin Chapman listens as Reine Wisell points out the change in angle of the rear wing of his car; Dan Gurney waits for team members to start his McLaren Can-Am car with an external battery; the Martini & Rossi 1971 long-distance team, left to right: Gerrard Larrousse, a friend, Vic Elford, Helmut Marko, and Gijs van Lennep; Jack Brabham in an aside to Ron Tauranac.*

Clockwise from above: Ferrari engineer Mario Forghieri seems stumped by a problem at the Canadian Grand Prix; John Surtees's mechanic examines a rear hub on the McLaren Formula I car; Frank Williams, left, briefs Tim Schenken; teammates Peter Gethin, left, and Denny Hulme; the hands of Sweden's Ronnie Peterson describe the March's behavior to a mechanic.

Top: *The Vic Elford–Kurt Ahrens long-tailed 917 Porsche is pushed away, its engine having failed after 19 hours of racing at Le Mans.* Above: *A privately entered Porsche 908 under unusually blue skies at the Nürburgring, 1971.*

Above: *Mario Andretti, left, and Jacky Ickx, enjoy their triumph in the six-hour race at Watkins Glen, 1972.*

would not be where he is. The mechanic realizes that a lesser driver might not have guided his machine safely through the race. There is a certain sense of gratitude a mechanic feels for a driver for having used the machine the way it should have been used and for making worthwhile the mechanic's extra hours of toil.

The rapport that builds up between mechanics and drivers is more than friendship. The driver places his life in the hands of the mechanic, and the mechanic knows the job must be done well and thoroughly. When Jo Siffert was killed at Brands Hatch in 1971, it was a mechanic, Siffert's personal mechanic and long-time friend, who walked at the head of the funeral procession, carrying Siffert's well-known helmet with the red and white Swiss cross.

The large international racing teams are blends of national types—English, American, German, Italian. In the pits it's bread and wine, a cup of tea heated with a blowtorch, hamburgers, and just enough of a common language to do the job right—or to talk to the native girls.

A mechanic travels a lot. The accommodations are sufficient, if not always first class. There's the airplane ticket, the rented car waiting at the airport, and the motel room, and the whole thing costs the mechanic nothing. He's getting paid to travel. There are different countries, different foods, new friends. But after a few years at it, the mechanic may feel that the pressure's too much. Then he may settle down with a garage of his own.

At many races the car's designer is present (especially if his creation is in its infancy):

Derek Gardner–Tyrrell, Mario Forghieri–Ferrari, Bruce Coppuck–McLaren, Robin Herd–March, Tony Southgate–first BRM and now with his new "Shadow." With the master himself on hand, new parts can be designed on the spot and tested.

Maybe those new principles and theories are not quite adaptable to this track; modifications must be made quickly. From Porsche, Ferrari, and Cosworth come the engineers with an ear for a cough or sputter. Depending on the intensity of the program and the amount a company or factory is willing to put into its effort, there is a range of engineers' support equipment. When Ford attacked Le Mans in the mid-sixties, there were immense trucks that housed complete machine shops, facilities to fabricate virtually anything needed. It was nearly the same with Porsche in the years 1968–71.

Behind the mechanics, engineers, and designer, all at work in the pits, are the timers and scorers. On large teams the timers and scorers are specialists. On smaller teams they could be wives or friends, but to be useful, they must have accuracy and concentration, because the changes that are made on the car in practice are directly based on the fluctuations in the times, fluctuations of fractions of a second. During the race it is essential that the scorers keep exact track of a car's position in the race. A driver must know in terms of seconds how far he is ahead of the car behind him and how far behind the car ahead. Thus he'll know just what he has to do to stay where he is and what he has to do to gain a place.

Everybody in the pits is armed with a stopwatch, of course, but time is officially

kept for the large teams by special chronographs. The manufacturer's decal is omnipresent on the cars and in the pits. The timer's precious chronograph usually doesn't travel with the rest of the luggage; the timer keeps it himself. One sees the timers on the plane or airport bus, their cases at their sides.

This then, is the core team of men who get a race car and its driver out on the track, in front, and first across the finish line. It is, doubtless, the largest support team in any sport, and beyond the core team, the retinue extends even further. There are the technicians supplied the teams by all the companies whose products the team uses—tire companies, brake-lining companies, gearbox manufacturers, headlight companies.

There are the organizers of the racing events—businessmen whose concerns are generally much wider than the managing of a race track since most race tracks are idle for the great part of the year.

There is the whole superstructure of people who govern the sport—track stewards, inspectors, officials, representatives of the several motor sports organizations, which may have a hand in making rules and policies for any race.

There are the promotional teams that are sent by the racing teams' sponsors and that keep busy around the track, handing out free samples and getting their scantily clad girls seen and photographed and their drivers interviewed. These interviews, though sometimes less than helpful to the team, are accepted with good grace.

The work of the core team is what gets the car into the winner's circle, but on race

day it's really the driver who is the star. There should be nothing to distract him from a smooth, efficient race, interspersed with fast, trouble-free pit stops. And that's the way it will be if the team has done its work properly in the months of testing, practicing and qualifying that come before the race. During those laborious days, the whole team is the star. Few people are looking, and hard work is far more important than glamour and guts.

4
SORTING IT OUT:
Practice and Qualifying

The track is empty. The grandstands echo like a deserted amphitheater to the sound of a single racing engine being revved. It roars, then dies. Nothing happens for a half an hour. Then the huge sound bellows again, and a racing machine heads tentatively onto the track to begin a solitary circuit. After one lap it comes in, the engine dies, and another hour of silence passes.

Racing is supposed to be the sport of speed and thrills, but testing is neither particularly speedy nor thrilling. It is, however, absolutely essential. Testing is the part of the sport that compares to theater auditions— early rehearsals in empty halls, an actor in street clothes, book in hand. The public is very rarely allowed in and would be bored to tears if it were. A good driver would no more miss a chance to test a car weeks before a race than a good actor would miss rehearsal. And the best drivers give just as much when the stands are empty as when a race is going on.

You'd think that maybe you'd have a tendency to give just a little more when there are people looking, but I can parallel a performance in, say, qualifying for Indy, where you have a hundred thousand people watching, with a tire test, where the whole place is empty. I feel that somehow—and I don't know why—I give it just as much when I'm tire testing. When I'm behind the wheel, it just seems that the competitive spirit comes out in me. You might think that there would be a difference in the way you drive, but in my opinion there isn't, at least not with the top people in the business. I feel that when and if

Dusk at Le Mans, and a long-tailed 917 moves under the Dunlop Bridge during night practice.

Above: *Jackie Stewart at Monaco.* Opposite: *Jo Siffert in the Yardley BRM during practice for the Dutch Grand Prix, 1971.*

I lose that drive, that ego trip within me, then I'll quit racing, period. It's not going to be when the fan letters stop coming in.—Mario Andretti

The degree of secrecy that surrounds a test varies. If the team is only grinding up tires to find out which compound will work best for a particular track, that's not particularly hush-hush. But if a new car, a new engine, or new aerodynamics are making a debut, then things tend to clam up.

For absolute secrecy, of course, the private test track is best—if you can afford one. Ferrari has one, newly designed, outside Milan in Maranello. Part of the new design is a series of television cameras, which are focused on each corner from several angles. Engineers sit in the comfort of the main control room and analyze the characteristics of the suspension as the car negotiates each turn. Porsche's private test facility is in Weissach, outside Stuttgart. It was here that the turbocharged 917-10 Can-Am car was nursed through its infancy. It emerged, eventually, a full-fledged, proven race car before it had ever turned its wheels in a race.

There are a few private test facilities that are not owned by huge corporations. One of the most private is Rattlesnake Raceway, Jim Hall's personal track. Mail goes to a post office box in Midland, Texas, but in fact the raceway is in the middle of the desert. It was here that the aerodynamic rear wing was first tested for Hall's Chaparral. An occasional roadrunner was probably the only living thing, besides Hall's engineers, that saw the radical 2J "sucker car" first perform in 1970.

YARDLEY
BRM
YARDLEY B.R.M.
CHRONOGRAPH
HEUER
CHAMPION
9
YARDLEY
B.R.M.

Besides testing newly designed or re-designed cars, testing is equally important to prepare a particular car for a certain race. Every team that can afford it likes to take drivers and cars to a track well before practice starts to see what can be learned about this track vis-a-vis this car. It's expensive. Safety crews have to be on hand for a single car, and the track has to be opened. It costs a thousand dollars a day at Daytona, but it should be done. Sometimes, teams will go to great lengths to squeeze information from a weekend of testing. At Sebring in 1972, a weekend was allotted for practice. Ferrari was there.

We sent down a car, five mechanics, engineers, and two drivers. Mario Andretti was the main test driver because he knows the track so well. We also sent Brian Redman in case Andretti felt ill or something else happened.

Now, Andretti goes out and sets the car up as he likes it, but he is also racing against the watch. You know you can't cheat the watch. The watch tells you whether you are faster or not, because often a driver is unable to tell if a change actually makes the car any faster. Many times he may actually feel that the car is going slower, but a glance at the watch will give the true picture.

For Sebring test weekend, I wasn't at Sebring but back at Modena. After each session the engineer, Giacomo Caliri, phones or sends a telex back to the factory, telling how many laps were done, top speeds, gear ratios used, tires, fuel consumption, tire wear, brake linings, and all that sort of stuff. With this information we can catalogue all the cars. When official practice starts, we have a definite place to start.—Peter Schetty

Testing before a race involves a crew, a car, drivers, and engineers. It's nothing, however, to what is required when the team packs up for the actual race. Three or four cars are not unusual in endurance racing. There must be two or three engines for every car—one for practice, one for the race, and a spare. A huge crew of mechanics and engineers, sponsors' representatives, public-relations

Clockwise from top: *Aligning lights during practice for Sebring; with new brake pads, a note to the driver to pump his brakes to wear them in; Vic Elford waits while a mechanic makes some adjustments on his car.*

people, wives, and guests are there. Tools and machinery, almost enough for building a new car on the spot, must go. Vans for hauling, eating out of, sometimes sleeping in, are essential. It's somewhat like a Broadway show going on the road and a floating automotive engineering college, all of it geared by the team manager specifically for the requirements of the particular race.

Take Sebring for example. The heat can usually be counted on to present all sorts of problems. It means you have to think about extra cooling for the water, oil, brakes, and drivers. Sebring is also a place where plenty of extra body pieces are needed because the track is only temporary and set up each year on runways. There are rubber cones that are used to mark the track, and as the race progresses, these cones are

knocked all over the track. Often, the drivers of the fast, low-to-the-ground prototypes hit these pylons at high speed, especially at night, and the cones can tear apart the front bodywork on fragile cars.

Now, for the Targa Florio, which is run on regular roads and where one lap is around seventy-two kilometers [forty-four miles], the team manager must think of other problems. Because of the length of the track, a spare wheel and jack must be carried in the car. In this case it's probably quicker for a driver to get out of his car and change the tire himself rather than limp back to the pits. Also, arrangements have to be made in advance for all the team's needs—fuel, oil, tires, and whatever other equipment and parts that are to be supplied by a sponsor.—P.S.

With everything packed and arrangements made for all equipment to be at the track when the team arrives, there remains the problem of getting there. Every mile of road between the team's shops and the track is a possibility for disaster. More than once, a car has been written off when its transporter was involved in an accident. In 1970, the radical Shadow Can-Am car was demolished when its transporter went off the road and over-turned. Emerson Fittipaldi's Lotus 72, the car that had carried him into the lead in the 1972 driving championship, met a similar fate on its way to the Italian Grand Prix. Luckily, Emerson's spare car was in another vehicle, and though it was well-used and tired, it lasted well enough for Emerson to win the race and clinch the championship.

With care accidents are for the most part preventable, but there's little the team can do to circumvent another barrier—the countries' borders. The transporters and all the equipment and cars within are at the mercy of customs officials. Experience teaches team managers to expect some sort of delay at the frontiers, but no experience can teach patience at the Spanish border. Practice has often been delayed at Spanish tracks because the trans-porters carrying the tires were held up at the border by a testy official. It would seem that organizers of Spanish racing events could arrange for teams and support personnel to cross the border more easily. As it is, team managers planning for any race in the Iberian Peninsula add an extra day for elaborate hag-

gling, paper stamping, and general confusion.

Once over the border and through customs, the teams finally arrive at the track. They are very often not the first to arrive. Already present is the army of advertising men and representatives of companies that are sponsoring teams, supplying free fuel or tires, or even staging the race itself. The track has already flowered from a drab grandstand beside a bit of twisting road into a panoply of banners, suitable decoration for the site of a medieval joust. Advertising is in place, designed not only for the spectators, who are beginning to assemble, but for the accidental glance of a camera. Already, television crews

are setting up, movie crews are roaming, and the still photographers are hard at work.

Most of this takes place in the pits and in the "paddock" area immediately behind the pits. (Automobile racing in the beginning borrowed lingo from horse racing.) The caravans of teams are packed in this area between the tents and huts erected by the sponsors, the advertisers, and the media crews, and the whole place takes on the air of a wealthy and hectic gypsy camp.

And then practice gets under way.

Everybody—spectators, advertisers, sponsors—is happy to stretch the racing event over the three or four days of practice rather than to be satisfied with the mere one day that the race itself is held. But just what is practice for besides the show? What is accomplished?

Basically, practice makes perfect. The more times you go around a track, the faster you'll go, the better the car can be adjusted, the more controlled your race will be. If every race track were a simple oval, like horse-racing tracks, extensive practice would obviously be far less necessary. But in international racing tracks come in every size, shape, length, condition, and quality. To know one is not to know them all.

Daytona is probably the most difficult race from the driver's point of view and from the engineer's because the banking poses very special problems for both. The problem is that in order for the car to handle fast and safely on the banking, it's impossible to have it handling well on the infield. The banking is very fast, with the car running flat out the whole time at very high speeds

—up to over two hundred miles per hour. On the infield all the corners are slow—second- or third-gear corners. So when you set up the car in an understeering situation, where it will handle safely on the banking, it simply won't go around the corners in the infield. We've tried doing it the other way so the car will handle well in the infield, but then it becomes almost undriveable on the banking. You get into the banking, and the car immediately gets sideways. There's always a certain amount of psychological problem for the drivers on the banking because the G-forces are so high; every lap it requires a little bit of screwing up of courage as you approach the second banking after the long straight, when the car is running absolutely flat out, to keep your foot to the floor on the accelerator.—Vic Elford

Daytona is basically an oval stock car track, with a few wiggles put into the infield to

Opposite: *Reine Wisell in a Lotus, foreground, and Jo Siffert make a few fast laps during practice before the rains come.* Top: *Out in the country at the Targa Florio in Sicily.* Bottom: *George Eaton in the North American Racing Team (NART) 512 at Le Mans during a practice session.*

make it like a road course when the sports cars come. The Nürburgring in Germany is utterly different. It may be the most challenging closed circuit in the sport. It's so well-planned, so thoroughly professional, that the myth has grown that it was built as a showpiece of German racing by Hitler. Actually, although the well-drilled teams of Auto Union and Mercedes-Benz did very well there during the thirties, the track was built as a public works project during the Weimar Republic. It's been changed now. It's less difficult, safer, and perhaps not quite as much fun. But there is one factor that holds a driver's interest.

I can remember being at the Nürburgring more than once when, in four days, it snowed, it hailed, there was fog, and even a little sunshine. Weather poses a problem during the race, even during practice. Often, practice times are un-

127

realistic. If it's been raining and stops and dries out for a moment, the driver who happens to get out and do a few laps before it starts to pour again is likely to find himself on the front row of the grid.—V.E.

For a whole new set of difficulties, try Sebring. It's an old airport whose runways and service roads are marked off into a temporary circuit with cones and hay bales. Unlike the European tracks it's completely flat. The track is very difficult to memorize because all parts of it look the same. During practice, drivers new to the track sometimes shoot off into the wrong road. At least there's usually space enough to spin off if you lose control. Also, it's hot; the Florida sun beats down on all that asphalt, and track temperatures reach 120 degrees. The race is 12 hours long and very punishing. Since it begins at 11 in the morning, it requires 5 hours of night driving.

Sebring is particularly difficult to drive at night. For this reason it is extremely important that the lights be adjusted properly. One of the problems with the lights is that under hard braking the height of the lights changes considerably. This was a problem we had to cope with.—P.S.

Most tracks on which the teams practice are built only for racing. Safety facilities line the track, there are guard rails, and the track is short enough to be committed to memory in the time allotted for practice. It wasn't always that way, at least not in European road racing, and, in the very old days, not in Grand Prix racing either. Races were held on

stretches of open road, which were linked to make a circular track and closed off for the day's racing. One of the few such major races left is the Circuito della Madonie in Sicily. These are the Sicilian roads along which is run the oldest continuing road race in Europe, the Targa Florio.

The roads are closed for about six or seven hours of practice a few days before the race and on race day itself. The rest of the practice time has to be done on open roads with people and trucks and buses and donkeys all over the place. We generally do our open-road practice from six in the morning till six at night, but I know one or two drivers who have practiced at night! Obviously, because of its length, the most difficult thing is to learn the circuit. I would say that probably there are only six or eight drivers of the many hundreds who have driven there that know the circuit intimately and totally.—V.E.

Opposite: *Andrea de Adamich negotiates a bridge during practice on the Targa Florio circuit.* Right: *More Targa Florio practice.* Bottom: *A man, his dog, and his donkey are often the only spectators during practice.*

Vic himself is one of those few. His years as a rally driver no doubt helped him memorize the track. The other driver noted for knowing the Targa intimately is Nino Vaccarella, who is a local schoolteacher and drives in very few other races but never misses a Targa Florio. He is usually among the top lappers. Vic Elford is one of the mere handful of non-Italians who have ever won the Targa. Obviously, it helps to be near enough to the track to drive it a lot.

In the villages there is always a possibility that someone will walk across the road in front of you, even when the road is closed and the race is on! Out in the countryside, the general daytime practice is invariably lightened by instances of running into flocks of sheep which block the road and hearty near misses with large trucks and buses. The road is very narrow anyway, and if a driver is practicing at anywhere near a respectable speed, he tends to cut corners and find himself on the wrong side of the road now and then. Incredibly, very few serious accidents happen. —V.E.

These four tracks—Daytona with its banks, Nürburgring with its weather, Sebring with the old runways, and Targa with its mountain roads and sheep—are not by any means extremes. Every track is different, so when the teams finally knuckle down to practice, there are a host of problems.

The car arrives at the track in a fairly neutral state in terms of handling characteristics; it neither understeers nor oversteers, it's neither "hard" nor "soft." These suspension settings are noted. Wing angles, tire pressure, and the adjustment of every adjustable piece of equipment on the car are catalogued by the team manager and chief mechanic. Then the driver sets out to custom tailor the car to himself and to the track. As has already been mentioned, the car is designed for the body of the man who will drive it or, in long-distance racing, the two or even three men who will drive it. Now, at the track this rough match is refined. Pieces of foam rubber and padding are put in or taken out, propping this up, bracing that. The driver is strapped in and goes out on his first practice lap. This is where "sorting it out" really begins.

Usually, in a sports car team where two drivers are used, the one with the most experience starts practice. This means that he starts practice with new tires, new brakes, new engine, and new everything.—P.S.

Lights on at dusk! A Porsche 917, top, and a Ferrari 512, bottom, at Le Mans.

The engine comes next. How does the engine feel as the car accelerates through the gears? Is it pulling smoothly all the way? The feeling you should get behind the wheel of a properly performing race car is instant power —foot down on the accelerator, the seat wraps around you, and the car plunges forward. It's been said that an ordinary driver would not be able to leave the pits in a Grand Prix car; the revs are so high that most people, even if they managed to avoid destroying the clutch on the first shift, would be unable to shoot out of the pits in a straight line, so sudden is the acceleration.

The steering—is it quick, responsive? A mere twitch, little more than a thought, and the car darts to right or left.

The brakes—are they firm and authoritative, reining in the car from 200 miles per hour to near nothing in near nothing flat? You can feel it, partly, by the pressure of your re-straining harness.

The tires and suspension through the corners—is the car breaking loose, oversteering, understeering, swaying, chattering, bobbing, or weaving? None of the above? All of the above?

Then the power full on for the straight again—but was that a miss in the engine at 6,500 r.p.m.? Yes—there it is again in third gear. Now how about fourth? No, it's not there. So around again, listening, hoping that the short bobble in the power curve will be there again. Far better to deal with it now, in practice, than to have it appear during the race.

Now the brakes again. This time they seem to be pulling to the right, to the left. The steering feels funny. So into the pits with a mental list of complaints for the team manager.

Now the changes start. Small adjustments— damper settings, tire pressures, different gear ratios, fuel injection adjustments. At Sebring in particular, where the weather is generally hot and dry, it is important to have the proper fuel injection settings. Perhaps the first driver is happy with the car, and he has gotten down to a competitive time. Then the other driver goes out in the car, does a few laps, comes in, and tells me how he likes it. Then the two drivers speak together, and we listen to see how far apart they are in their likes and dislikes. In team driving there are always compromises.—P.S.

This process is somewhat easier if both drivers are knowledgeable about what is going on under the hood and in the suspension of their cars. A few of them are expert mechanics,

130

but many of them have a lot of difficulty translating what they felt was wrong with the car into instructions a mechanic can follow. One of the team manager's tasks is to act as interpreter between drivers and mechanics and sometimes between driver and driver. In international racing it's not unusual for a team to have drivers and mechanics who share no common language, much less a common viewpoint as to what should be done to the car. This language problem no doubt added a small irritant to Alfa Romeo's big problems during the 1972 season. The chief engineer, Carlo Chiti, spoke no English but only Italian and French; Vic Elford, only English and French; Helmut Marko, only English and German; and several of the drivers, only Italian. Only one of the engineers spoke English and his was far from perfect.

One of Peter Schetty's advantages as a team manager was his polyglot abilities—as a Swiss he spoke perfect French, German, English, and Italian. Beyond that he became adept at translating "driverese" into terms that a mechanic could understand. Having a degree in engineering and having been a prototype driver obviously helped.

The drivers are not engineers, or at least in most cases they are not. I have to talk with the driver and see how he feels about the setups on the car. Sometimes the driver explains himself mostly in sign language, which is not much help to the mechanic or engineer. I understand what the driver means when he expresses himself. Then I translate this into a change in a spring rate or a replacement of a shock absorber or sway bar.—P.S.

Despite the exactness with which a team manager can translate driver's feelings into changes, a great deal of work that is done on the car during a practice session is trial-and-error adjustment. Careful comparisons are made between lap times and engine r.p.m. whenever the slightest change is made. A wing is raised or lowered by millimeters.

Out on the track, the engine is 300 r.p.m. lower on the long straights than it was. But the lap times turn out to be a fraction of a second better. Although the driver is losing time on the straight, he is more than making up for it in the corners because there is more downward force on the wing. The change stays.

It's very important then that the driver turn in consistent laps during practice. The only gauge available to the team is the driver. He knows if he is driving the track in basically the same manner with one setup as with another. Driving consistently is almost more important than describing whether the car felt better or worse; those subjective feelings can be discounted if lap times tell a different story.

In a race, the competition is with other cars. You know exactly who is ahead and who is behind you, where you stand, and what you have to do to catch up and win. In practice, though, you're racing against only the stopwatch, and when you're out on the track, you can't see it. You have no way of knowing, beyond your own feelings and until you pull into the pits and see the team manager, whether you are going as fast as you can. For the driver, practice is really a race against himself, with the stopwatch as umpire.

There are two limits—the car's and the driver's. The car's limit is somewhat more

131

Below: *Braking point markers for the esses at Le Mans. Opposite: Ferrari 312, Arturo Merzario at the wheel, at the Dutch Grand Prix.*

definite, but there's no sure way you can tell when it has been reached. The driver's limit is much more subjective and can change with time, mood, and years.

When the speeds go up, it's not that the human element is getting better, really, as an average. It's just that the cars are capable of going faster. So I go as fast as I can, and beyond that, well, I'm just not going to find out. I think I'm a better driver than I ever was. I still have the same drive to win as I ever did. I just don't have stars in my eyes anymore.—M.A.

Practice is about limits—the limits of the car and the limits of its driver at this track on this day. The braking point marks the limit that must be found, a limit that is a nexus of man's ability and machine's. At some tracks, organizers have been thoughtful enough to put up distance markers—300, 200, 100 feet to the apex of the turn. But at many other tracks, the braking point must be an arbitrary landmark—

a stump, a rock, a patch in the pavement, or a heartbeat after that patch or that rock.

At first, the driver narrows down the braking point to a specific area—between two distance markers or between the rock and the stump. You go a little farther before braking the next time and then a little farther still until you find the point at which it is simply too late. Then you lock up the brake, and the car gets sideways. You straighten out, but you've lost time. Now you work on braking that late but *not* losing control, and if you succeed you move a little closer to the curve before lifting your foot from the accelerator, pumping the brake pedal, and wrestling with the wheel.

And you spin again. You've found the braking point—the point on that curve beyond which neither you nor your car can go. It's one braking point back.

Then the next curve. . .

That's all fine for practice when you have no other cars around you, breathing down your neck, darting in and out, trying to slide inside

132

you. And it's fine when you can see that patch, rock or stump. But what do you do when you tear into a corner in a race in the middle of a pack of sliding, weaving, fire-eating, smoke-belching monsters all lunging for the same turn? Then you'd better have done your work well, and that practice braking point had better have become reflexive.

Then there is that mysterious geometry lesson race drivers are always talking about—the "proper line." Where is that line that is the quickest way through the corner, that leaves you with the best shot at the straight that follows? It could be worked out and measured and painted on the road for the driver to follow, but that would ruin some of the sport. Instead, the driver has to experiment.

First, attack from the left, turn into the corner, clip the side of the road with the front tire, and then shoot out the other side. But you run out of road and have to struggle to change direction. You've lost time. The next time, you go a little earlier on the entry so as to have enough road to drive out on, but you miss the apex of the turn, so that's no good. You try over and over until the line is down.

The right speed along that line must be reached. The car must be set up to drift, that is, it must be driven fast enough into the corner and turned suddenly enough so that it will actually move crablike through the turn until it's facing out and the power is applied again. To do this, the car has to be driven into the corner faster than it should be. It has to be thrown into a sort of controlled out-of-control. The faster the corner, the more courage is required to drift through it.

The high-speed drift is really where the driver finds his limit. With braking points, you know at least that whenever you must, you can apply the brakes and that you are in control. But the fast, fourth- or fifth-gear corner is where you're really balancing on the high wire. Your speed must be right; your line must be right. A deviation in either, and you can be thrown into a spin in the path of a following car or off the track into a guard rail or an earth bank. That's called "having a moment." "I had a moment out there when the suspension upright broke." The car was drifting just barely under control through a curve at 180 miles per hour!

Again, practice isn't the race. It's one thing to manage a high-speed drift alone, quite another to manage it when you're flying in formation with five or six other cars, all with the same intention.

It may sound as if practice is quite a reasonable process of discovering certain geometrical and mechanical facts and functions without the stress of competition. Not so. Practice can be dangerous, maddening, and very destructive. In manufacturers' championship racing, there are all kinds of cars out on the track—slow, fast, ponderous, agile—and drivers to match. There are always local entries and inexperienced men, who are not really in control of their cars. That can be frightening. Many are the bumps, nicks, angry looks, and curses drowned in the roar of the engines.

Various tracks have various obstacles for a driver out to learn the track. The Targa Florio has already been mentioned.

When I first came here in 1967, I did forty minutes [on a forty-four mile track] on open roads with a Carrera 6. It was about six o'clock in the morning, and I just didn't see anything, so I got braver and braver, and eventually, I was taking the proper line. I only went about three minutes quicker in the race, with the 910.—V.E.

In a lot of motor racing, the cars that are quickest either in practice or during special qualifying laps start the race at the top of the lineup, or grid. Depending on the kind of race, this positioning can be very important or not important at all. For long-distance racing, it's pretty meaningless, and it's more a matter of pride than usefulness that makes individuals battle each other and the clock for top starting position. Jacky Ickx cared so little about where his car started the 1969 24 Hours of Le Mans that when the starter was dropping the green flag, Ickx was still on his way out to get in his car.

It's quite different in sprint races such as the races of the world driving championship, the Grand Prix races. These are short races, all the cars are pretty well matched, there is really no "traffic" of cars out to win lesser classes or just have fun going around the track, all the drivers theoretically have some chance, and the races are often won by fractions-of-a-second differences in lap times. If a poor qualifying time puts a driver back in the pack, he must first catch the cars that started first and second. It may be eight or ten laps before he is able to maneuver past the cars directly in front of him. By this time the lead cars have piled up an almost insurmountable lead.

In the 1972 Grand Prix at Monaco, Jean-Pierre Beltoise was able to rocket into the lead from the second row of the grid. Because the track was soaked by a downpour, he was the only car to have a clear view of the track. The cars behind him not only had to adapt to the wet conditions but had to fight the blinding spray thrown up by Beltoise.

In Grand Prix racing, a lead of a few seconds early in the race often cannot be

Right: *François Cevert in the Tyrrell at Monaco. Below: Jo Siffert at the Nürburgring in his Porsche 908.*

taken away from you, and if you're on the pole or in the first row, you have a chance to grab those seconds early. During the last laps of practice at Watkins Glen in the 1972 U.S. Grand Prix, Jackie Stewart performed a ritual that only a few understood. As he passed the pits and headed for the first turn, a sharp 90-degree right-hander, Stewart swung to the right inside of the track, off the regular line itself. Great clouds of dust and pebbles were thrown up. Stewart had the pole position, and if he could prevent it, nobody was going to reach that first turn before he did. To ensure it, he was clearing a path for himself and finding a braking point that he could use only once—on the first lap.

At the drop of the flag, Stewart pulled to the inside instantly, flew down the line he had marked on the inside edge of the track to the first turn, and was easily first through the turn. With that advantage, he began to pull away from the field from the start and came home an easy winner.

For many persons starting in racing, the mechanics of a car are all difficult to understand.

But the more racing you do, the more you learn about the workings. In testing you learn quite a lot, and little by little you understand about tires and suspension and gearing. The more you learn about the mechanical aspects of a car, the more you understand how crucial suspensions, gearboxes, tires, and so forth are. If you are driving on a team, for example, and the day before, the suspension has broken on another car, it's not very nice, because on long straights sometimes you think about the same thing happening on your car. Sometimes, it's not so good to know all about the car!—P.S.

Knowing about the car gives you some patience during practice, a virtue that not many drivers have. The machinery that today's drivers work with is complex, and the time needed to pamper it into giving its best often taxes the nerves.

On the verge of a fast practice lap, the accelerator sticks. Into the pits. The mechanics work on the problem. Then back out again. For three laps everything's fine. Then, in the middle of the fast lap, it sticks again. Back to the pits, where closer examination reveals that

the problem is more extensive than it had appeared. For the remainder of the session, the driver has to occupy himself while the others are honing their cars lap after lap and learning the track. To the fans that crowd the paddock area and know little of what's going on with the car, it seems that most of every practice session is spent idly—shop talk, business talk, car talk, interviews, autographs, pictures.

One thing a top driver has to get used to is a camera lens. In no other sport is the participant more closely under photographic fire than in racing, perhaps because a driver must spend so much time sitting around in uniform. And then there are the microphone people with endless questions. Why do you race? (*Why not?*) What do you think of Ferrari driver X? (*I think he's a mad clown, but I'm damned if I'm going to tell you that.*) How do you like your car? (*Fine. I wish I was in it now instead of talking to you.*)

You know, to be famous is sometimes good. It helps you to get things. But if you have to stay late and sign autographs and answer questions and so on, and if you can't go home until eight o'clock every night, well, that can be very difficult sometimes.—Helmut Marko

In no other sport is there the direct commercial interest that there is in racing. Large companies use racing to advertise their products—tires, spark plugs, fuel—either because these products supposedly help a car to go faster or better or merely because a team or driver agrees to have the name painted on cars and uniforms. So there is an immense amount of public-relations money invested in the race, and it becomes a full-fledged sideshow in the paddock area—very festive, it must be admitted. The pop art of advertising is shown to best advantage in conjunction with the hard-edged art of modern racing machinery.

Beyond the straightforward posters and banners, the advertisers fit out tents, reception areas, clubs—whatever they feel is required to give their product prestige with drivers and crowd. Maybe its a gaggle of girls in matching outfits handing out free samples. Yardley cosmetics, Martini & Rossi, and Champion have all sent armies of beauties to saturate a track with samples. And there's nothing like

a free sample from the Moet et Chandon booth.

The drivers often figure largely in the promotional campaign. It's the price they often must pay for sponsorship, and this extremely expensive sport would die without sponsors. Most drivers realize that. The sponsors that a driver personally allows to put their names on his uniform (cigarette companies, banned from television, are devotees of this kind of walking poster) are not only paying the driver,

but also very often helping to pay the huge bills that a driver's team is accumulating.

It's no good pretending that we're just racing drivers and we just sort of arrive at the track with our crash helmets, drive a car, and then go home or to a pub afterward. I think the racing driver of thirty or forty years ago was the sort of rich young gentleman who just wanted something he could do with his money to enjoy himself, whereas

138

now motor racing is a highly professional sport —and it's very much the entertainment business, in fact. There's a lot more to motor racing now— partly politics, the commercialism involved. Racing drivers have got a lot of responsibility to other people in terms of the money that's being put in. Some of it can be a bit tedious, but on the whole I think most drivers enjoy it.—V.E.

They'd better. There's no better time than practice for the sponsors to squeeze promotional advantage out of their contracted drivers, mostly because while his car is being worked on, the driver has little to do but stroll around the paddock area, displaying his decals and being photographed. It all creates a particular difficulty for the driver. When the driver gets in his car to practice, he is all race driver, but when he climbs out, he is a celebrity, an authority on the sport, and a representative of three or four corporations as well. He has to be able to turn his concentration on and off during practice. Otherwise he won't be able to think solely about the car; he'll still be dwelling on some conversation he had with a potential sponsor a few minutes before.

It's no good saying that the drivers should be isolated from this prying public and promotion-hungry sponsor for the two or three days of practice. If practice (and the race, for that matter) were not the advertising circus it is, there wouldn't be the money to put the best drivers into the best cars on the best-prepared tracks. And that is what racing is all about.

Because race drivers are the kind of people they are, there are contests within contests during practice. There is a fight for the fastest time during practice, for the fastest

time of the day, even for the fastest time of each session. After each session there is usually a printed time sheet. It's like having your grades publicly posted at school. A driver's problems during practice aren't mentioned; only his achievement is posted on the main bulletin board. It may be eight seconds slower than a comparable car, but those who read the time don't realize that his car was understeering terribly or that the engine was missing in right-hand turns or that there was a flock of other things that were keeping him from a good performance.

This is the driver's livelihood that the fates are playing with. Probably the hardest thing a driver must do is dismiss the word "if" from his vocabulary. After an excellent start in the 1972 Targa Florio, Vic Elford had to withdraw when his engine expired out on the circuit.

It's no good saying I would have won the Targa Florio if I'd finished. I didn't finish, and I didn't win, and nobody's going to remember next year what happened to me. They're only going to remember that Merzario and Munari won the race. The only thing that matters, really, is who wins and what goes in the record books.—V.E.

You finish poorly because you had problems during practice, which put you far back in the pack at the start of the race, which in turn caused you to be in the first-lap pileup, which flattened a tire and caused a lengthy limp back to the pits, which lost time and precipitated a hopeless drive to the checkered flag. Everybody will sympathize, but what remains is that you didn't finish and you didn't win. That's what will be remembered.

5

THE CHECKERED FLAG:

The Race Itself

Few spectacles in sports compare in excitement to the start of an automobile race. Sports car driver Vic Elford, when asked what for him is the climax of the race, says simply, "The start."

For me winning is really an anticlimax. Depending on the race, you've been building up to that moment for a month, a week, a day, an afternoon. Suddenly it's all over, and if you've won, it doesn't seem all that exciting or dramatic. Perhaps your expectations as to the feeling of winning are greater in your mind than they are in actuality. For me the climax in racing is the start. That's the point at which you are at your highest level emotionally. After that your emotions change to mechanics, for the real business of driving a car and racing is mainly mechanical.
—Vic Elford

With the dawn of a race day, tension mounts as the hour of the start draws near. The race's long traditions, its importance in the series, its unknowns, only increase the electricity.

The prerace pageantry—the marching bands, the exhibition races, the speeches—are put on mainly for the spectators. They go unnoticed by those directly connected with the race. In the pits drivers in fireproof finery talk with competitors, friends, and reporters, trying to look at once natural and heroic as the Nikons and Instamatics are poked in their faces. "Mario! Mario! Over here, Mario!" Some drivers, escaping from the masses of people who manage to get into the pit and paddock area, withdraw to the relative quiet and privacy of the team van or garage.

The rainy start of the Dutch Grand Prix at Zandvoort in 1971.

You have to be understanding, like before a race. You know you'd rather be by yourself to think things out, but you can't really expect the layman to know what's going on inside you. You'd rather just snub them and say the hell with it, but instead you have to put up with these distractions and suffer just a little. Some guys start worrying the night before the race, but I figure you'll worry when the time comes. Worrying goes along with the job, because when things are uncertain you always worry. Every race is a brand new deal, a whole new ball game. That's the interesting part. You don't know what the outcome of the race will be, so what the hell. Obviously you're a little nervous over breakfast. You don't know how the day is going to end up. Each day like that is an important day. When you go into a race, you have strategy, but as the race progresses, you have to change and call the shots differently. That's all part of it.

Before the race I personally let the tension build up a bit for two or three hours so that by the time it starts I'm sort of in a high, nervous pitch. Some drivers let it build up all during the week prior to the race, but generally I try to be as relaxed as possible for as long as possible. It never seems to change very much. I always feel about the same before every race, although one race may be a little different than another. I feel particularly tense at Le Mans, because it's such a helluva long way and the chances of finishing are relatively small. But at most races I get a tightening in my stomach, and I don't really want to talk to anybody. Yet I have to keep moving.—Mario Andretti.

Team managers and mechanics scurry, tending to last-minute details on their cars, impatient with the crowd of fans and hangers-on. This is no holiday for them, and the responsibility they have is more than just doing well in a race.

As you walk around the busy pits, you can't help but think, if only for a moment, that the driver laughing and joking a few feet away may, within the hour, be trapped in a mass of tangled wreckage. Although the drivers take the greatest risk, it's not safe work for anyone close to it—mechanics, course workers, ambulance drivers.

The start is near. Cars are rolling out of their garages or pits for the formation of a grid. Drivers, anxious to slide behind the wheel, their faces more intent now, pull on their fireproof hoods and gloves. On the grid the cars are lined up two-by-two, three-by-three, or two-by-three-by-two. The faster cars are closest to the pole, the pole being the position on the starting line nearest to the first turn. Crew members force a few extra pints of fuel into their cars and check to see that wheels are tight and fittings are secure. The drivers climb in, fasten their elaborate harnesses, wait. . . .

Starts of major races today have been narrowed to two types—rolling, and stopped with engines running. The most widely used, probably because it is considered the safest, is the rolling start. In twos or threes, the drivers follow a pace car on a slow circuit of the track. Most drivers will take advantage of the pace lap to do two things—scrub their tires and bed their brakes. The drivers can be seen swerving erratically from side to side through the pace lap so that the new tires can be worn slightly and heated. A hot tire adheres to the

Pedro Rodriguez after winning the 1971 six-hour race at Watkins Glen in a Porsche 917 with Leo Kinnunen.

The grid being formed for the 1971 running of Le Mans.

Opposite: *A Porsche 917 and a Porsche 908 sweep down the long undulating straight at the Nürburgring 1,000-kilometer race, 1971. Left: Tony Adamowicz's North American Racing Team (NART) Ferrari 512 belches fire from its exhaust in the early morning of the 1971 Daytona 24-hour race. Bottom: The remains of Peter Revson's Lola after a tire came off the rim at the end of the straight, Road Atlanta, 1970.*

Above: American driver Tom Dutton jumps from his burning Can-Am car at Road Atlanta, 1970. Top: Martini & Rossi long-tailed Porsche 917, Vic Elford driving, leads the field on the pace lap at Le Mans, 1971. Right: Chris Amon in the Formula I Matra at Zandvoort, 1971.

Above: *Dusk at Le Mans, 1970.*
Below: *Dan Gurney, Sebring, 1970.*

Nino Vaccarella in an Alfa Romeo prototype sandwiched
between two local entries in the Sicilian countryside
during the Targa Florio, 1971.

Below: *Formula I cars bunch up at the start of the Monaco Grand Prix, 1971.* Right: *John Surtees practicing at Watkins Glen in one of the first cars to bear his name.* Bottom: *Jean-Pierre Beltoise in the French-blue Matra Formula I car flashes by the curbing at Monaco, 1971.*

Below: *Nino Vaccarella's winning Alfa Romeo Type 33 brakes for a turn in the town of Collesano during the 1971 Targa Florio.* Right: *The Martini & Rossi Porsche 917, which was driven to victory by Helmut Marko and Gijs van Lennep, at the Mulsanne corner, Le Mans, 1971.* Below right: *A Formula I car claws its way through a corner during the Dutch Grand Prix, Zandvoort, 1970.*

*Mario Andretti in a Ferrari 512 goes through the old loop
at Watkins Glen during the 1970 six-hour race.*

Opposite: *Waiting for the start at the Watkins Glen Can-Am race. In front, two McLaren M8Fs; behind, the Chaparral 2J "sucker" car and the Lola 222. Below: Peter Revson in the Sunoco Javelin leads the Mustang and Camaro team cars past the pits at St. Jovite, 1970.*

asphalt far better than a cool one, and by heating the tire on the pace lap, the driver increases his car's cornering ability for the mad dash through the first turn. The disc brakes, too, have to be broken in, or "bedded," so on the pace lap the driver sharply applies the brakes two or three times.

As the swerving, dashing, and braking field approaches the starting line, it forms two orderly lines and slows to a speed at which all cars are "on the cam," at a power–gear ratio at which the torque of the engine can be used to fullest advantage at the drop of the flag

The standing start with engines running is used at most Formula I or Grand Prix races. In order to allow these finely tuned engines to warm up to a temperature close to actual racing conditions, the cars are sent off on one circuit of the track after being gridded. This warm-up lap often uncovers problems in a

Opposite: *The start of the 1,000-kilometer race through the Eifel Mountains at the Nürburgring. Jacky Ickx in the Ferrari 312 leads into the first turn.* Left: *A few laps later, still leading but smoking badly.*

car or two, and mechanics of the ailing machines are allowed to work feverishly up to the start. Once the grid has reformed, the driver must coordinate his clutch and accelerator perfectly to unleash all the car's horsepower for the charge from the starting line. A stall at this point can cost a driver the entire race and can cause a massive rear-end accident.

The traditional "Le Mans start" with drivers sprinting to their cars has been abandoned in recent years for two reasons. The massive traffic jam of cars pulling out left and right often resulted in accidents when the race was seconds old. Also at Le Mans, being first around the corner and under the Dunlop Bridge used to be more important to some drivers than fastening their seat belts and shoulder harnesses when they got into their cars. It's possible that the first-lap death of Englishman John Woolfe at Le Mans would have been averted if he had been securely strapped into his Porsche 917 when it suddenly swerved off the track in 1969, the

last year the Le Mans start was used.

No matter how the cars start, the sound of engines, the smell of the oil, rubber, and gasoline burning, and the sight of thousands of dollars worth of machinery tearing away from the starting line sends chills through the most casual spectator. In the first few minutes of a race, the drivers usually proceed in a manner that can be described only as cautiously aggressive. They're feeling out the opposition, once again getting into the groove, reestablishing their braking points, and preparing mentally and physically for the next hours of racing. They're cautious because it's at the start of the race that the traffic is heaviest and the cars are closest. Six or seven cars are often bunched in a tight group, weaving back and forth, jockeying for position, and attempting to overtake cars by diving into the corners.

Let's assume that we have two drivers and two cars of similar caliber. When they take a

147

corner, they will both be taking it at about the limit of their own and their cars' abilities—not right at the limit but very close to it. If the car in front is taking the corner as fast as it's possible to take it, then it follows that the one behind can't possibly go any quicker around the corner and therefore can't overtake in the corner.

Now if one car is obviously faster than another, it is quite easy to overtake on sheer speed, but when the two are almost equally matched, the only solution is to slipstream. The car in back gets as close as possible to the car in front—perhaps three feet—and drafts it on the straight. By doing this the following car is sort of sucked along in the vortex of the lead car to such an extent that the driver of the car in the back can actually back off the throttle. When the car in front reaches its maximum speed, it just isn't going to go any faster. The car behind is going exactly the same speed, but the driver is not using all the throttle. He has a considerable amount of power left.

The technique is to sit there until the car in front has reached its maximum speed. Then you put your foot to the floor, and as the car leaps forward, you duck out from behind the car in front into the wind stream and hope that the speed you have built up is enough to slingshot you ahead. If you misjudge your leap, you'll just pull up alongside the car in front and go no farther in front since you are once again both going the same speed with the same amount of wind resistance.

The other method of overtaking is to outbrake the car you are racing with. Since both cars are going to go around the corner at the same speed and as fast as it is possible for them to go around, one of them must arrive at the corner first. Let's

say that you have the ability to keep up with the car you are trying to overtake or even perhaps get alongside. As you approach the corner, in the last few tenths of a second, one of you has got to give way to the other in order to take the proper line through the corner. At this point a great deal of the skill comes into racing—pushing yourself and your car to the limit to make sure that you are not the one who gives way, that you are the one who brakes last. You've got to screw up your courage. If there's a fence or a barrier waiting at the end of the corner, you've got to be able to convince yourself that you can wait until that very last moment to brake.

Normally, when a car is going to take a right-hand corner, it positions itself on the extreme left of the track so it can use the maximum amount of road and therefore make the straightest line— the fastest line—through the corner. But if you're trying to overtake, you're going to be inside the other car, which means that you have slightly less road to work with. Your ultimate speed around the corner is going to be a little bit slower than if you were using all the road. Somehow, you've got to push yourself beyond the car that you're trying to overtake. You've got to get into the corner first. When you get such a situation, the actual entry to the corner—after the two cars have fought to decide who's going to brake first—is quite untidy, because what has become important is not how fast you get around the corner, but whether you get into it before the other car.

In racing there is sort of a delicate code of ethics that deals with overtaking. Without it the competition in the corners would degenerate toward a series of batterings. If two cars come into a corner parallel or very close together, they both obviously have a lot of responsibility, but the car on the inside actually has more responsibility. Say both cars put their brakes on at the same time, but for one or reason or another, the car on the outside of the corner arrives at the corner first. Then the car on the inside has total responsibility for getting out of the way, because the other one is simply going to take his line through the corner, and if the inside car just simply stays there, they're going to collide.

If you're trying to pass a competitive car, it doesn't just happen at the first corner you come to. Depending on the race, you probably sit behind the car for twenty laps, working out how you're going to get past. Then you finally make your decision. Perhaps you find that there is a particular corner where the driver in front of you is not quite braking to the limit, that this would be a good place to overtake. Having made the decision to overtake on a particular corner, you spend two or three laps getting into the right sort of attacking position to do it. You have to be sure that you will be going at least as fast as the car ahead when you arrive at the corner to put the brakes on. You've got to be as close as you possibly can be to the car ahead. You may be going just slightly quicker as you reach the point that you brake, which will give you just enough impetus to get past.

If you are the pursued rather than the pursuer, there are a number of things that you can do to keep ahead. You can either try driving that little bit faster and waiting a little bit longer to brake because you know that in order for the car behind to pass, he must take an imperfect line and it will be difficult for him to brake and get through the corner without going off the road or spinning. You can also use different parts of the road that you normally wouldn't. The ideal line

Clockwise from right: *Alfa Romeo Type 33 in the pit; a Porsche 917 passes its street counterparts, 911s, at Le Mans, 1971, with a flash of its lights; a rainy start at Zandvoort.*

Below: *Larrousse out and Elford in during a pit stop at the Nürburgring that they won, 1971.* Opposite top: *A Penske pit stop during the Trans-Am race at St. Jovite, 1970.* Opposite bottom: *One of the John Wyer Gulf Porsche 917s in the pits at Monza, 1971.*

through a corner is from left to right on a right-hand corner and vice versa. But if you are just ahead of the car that is chasing you, you can completely control the corner by taking the incorrect line. Anyone wanting to go by will have to take the outside line, an almost impossible chore since you will have reached the corner first.

I know I wouldn't, and I don't know many people who would allow someone to overtake automatically. It's all part of racing to stay in front for as long as reasonably possible. Let's say that somebody else has a better or faster car than you

and is ahead of you on the grid for a Grand Prix, but you happen to make a better start and get in front of him. Well, you're not going to move over automatically and let him by. You could conceivably hold him off for the entire race. There is a fine line between racing with another car or just blocking him.—V.E.

In a two- or three-car team, one man might be sent out at the start as the hare, setting a blistering pace to lure the opposition into a chase, hoping that after two hours of

152

chasing, they'll find themselves in the pits, unable to match the hare's pace. The driver assigned the job of leading the chase also finds his mount gasping and choking and, his job done, retires.

After the first grueling laps of the race are completed and a driver has time to notice signals, the crews begin an elaborate ritual of flashing signals on a board as the car speeds by. The pit-board signal is as old as racing, but recently, a couple of teams began trying radio communication. The radio system was used very successfully during the 1971 Indianapolis 500 by the Johnny Lightning team with Al Unser driving. During practice and qualifying a two-way system was used, the driver being able to both hear and talk. For the race, though, chief mechanic George Bigniotti changed the system to one-way, driver to pit, since he felt a two-way radio might disturb Unser's concentration at the wrong time. During the race several accidents occurred on the far side of the track, and Unser described them in detail to his crew, listening in pit row.

Clockwise from right: *A long-tail Porsche leads two Ferrari 512s; Dave Walker in the Lotus turbine at Zandvoort, 1971; two Alfa Romeos on the banking at Daytona, Vic Elford and Andrea de Adamich driving; the start of the 24 Hours of Le Mans, 1971.*

With the old pit-board system, each team uses a code to communicate with its drivers. A message of some sort will be on the pit-board on almost every lap. Team managers can relay fairly complicated orders through the pit-boards, ask questions of their drivers, and, when a substantial lead allows, even joke with them. Most signals, of course, are the driver's lap time, his position in the race, the time remaining in the race, his time ahead or behind the nearest car, and orders to bring the car in for a pit stop.

Certain kinds of races are meant to be run start to finish without a pit stop for fuel, but in long-distance racing, these high-speed fueling operations allow crews to demonstrate just how fast it can be done. Roger Penske's team, in the Trans-Am series, has cut a 22-gallon fuel stop down to six seconds.

When a car arrives suddenly in the pits, unscheduled, there must be no confusion in diagnosing a problem and repairing it. The mechanics may be presented with a jammed shift lever, a short in the electrical system, a brake failure, or a slew of other mechanical ills. A classic instance of confusion in the pits was a stop by the late Mexican driving ace, Pedro Rodriguez, in the 1969 U.S. Grand Prix. He pulled in to change a badly chunked tire on his Ferrari. The factory crew quickly had the used tire off, but as it was rolled away toward the wall, it collided with the new one, which was being rolled in to be put on. The two tires danced around each other. When they settled, the frantic mechanic quickly grabbed what he thought was the new tire and slapped it on the car. Only the sharp eyes of a nearby spectator caught the error and pre-

154

vented Rodriguez from rejoining the fray on the used and badly chunked tire.

When he's working on a car that has been forced into the pits, a mechanic has to keep in mind that despite the urgency of getting the car back on the track as quickly as possible, a man's life is riding on the machinery that he's attempting to fix. The job must be done quickly, but it must also be done completely. Checking the condition of a partially damaged shock absorber may take a precious minute, but it could prevent a breakage and a subsequent sudden and violent loss of control.

There's also another, more immediate, danger that requires constant vigilance in the pits—fire. Hurried stops in racing can result in gasoline shooting out of the overflow and venting tubes. Most racing cars are equipped with disc brakes, and the chance of fuel spilling on a red-hot disc and erupting into flames is a distinct possibility. It has happened more than once. Crews of some cars are beginning to wear fireproof Nomex suits and face masks like those worn by the drivers themselves. Hundreds of gallons of gasoline are stockpiled in the pit area during a race, and a small

Opposite: *Townsfolk gather on a hill-side outside the town of Collesano during the running of the Targa Florio.* Top: *A Porsche 908 moves through the main street of the same town.* Right: *Not much safety between the cars and the crowd lining the street at this race.*

spark can easily set off a fire that could spread quickly with disastrous results.

In long-distance endurance racing, drivers change periodically during pit stops.

In sports car racing, it used to be that a top-of-the-line driver would be employed to drive the car, and the other driver was just responsible for turning adequate laps and bringing it back in one piece. In 1972, I was really the only one of the six drivers who was not a Formula I regular. I classify myself as a sports car driver, not a Formula I driver. Coming into the team at the beginning of

the year, I was pretty worried, because I thought the boys were going to show me up very badly. But in fact, I've held my own relatively well in this very strong team.

When I started sports car racing, the general pattern had been that sports car teams employed a number-one driver and a number-two driver, who was very much a backup, and it was understood that he wasn't as fast as the number-one driver. His job was to drive the car consistently and bring it back in one piece. Ferrari changed this in 1972 by employing nothing but number-one drivers.—Brian Redman

Below: *Ickx and Rodriguez are first away in the rain at Zandvoort, 1971.* Bottom: *Ronnie Bucknum in the Ferrari 512 he codrove with Tony Adamowicz to a second-place finish at Daytona, 1971. The car breathes fire on the second day of racing there.* Right: *Pedro Rodriguez in a Porsche.*

Like a stage manager giving the star his cue, the team manager alerts the codriver well before his car is due in if indeed the driver hasn't been waiting, expectantly, tensely, through his codriver's stint. He dresses in his fireproof suit, draws on his sweaty mask and gloves, tries to hear his team manager's advice and instructions over the engine roar, and watches along pit road for the car to come in. What's it like out there? How's the car? Is it different now than when he got out of it four hours ago? He knows whether his codriver has gained or lost time on the track, knows what he must do to keep in the contest. But how's the car? It comes in, the driver leaps out, and there's time for a few words—the track, the handling, third gear, a wreck on the hairpin. The new driver is into the still-warm seat, his harness is buckled, the team manager gives the signal, and the familiar roar

of the engine is around him once again.

Out on the track, breaks in traffic and stretches of straight road allow his thoughts to drift occasionally.

Often when you're charging down long straights with your foot planted to the floor at two hundred miles per hour, you think, "Christ, I wish I wasn't here. What if the tire blows?" You feel a vibration. You think, "What's that? Is something going to fall off? I wish I was home with the kids."

It depends on the situation. If you're really charging desperately hard, you don't have time to think because you have to look at the gauges every now and again and make sure everything's okay and concentrate on any funny noise or vibration. You just don't know. Maybe it's something, maybe it's nothing. You have to try to evaluate what it is and what you're going to do about it.—B.R.

Clockwise from top: *A Porsche 917 followed by a Ferrari 512 brakes for the Ford chicane at Le Mans; into the first turn at Daytona; downhill and into the esses at Le Mans goes the Matra of Beltoise and Amon.*

For the most part, then, the driver is busy driving, checking his instruments, and communicating with his pits. For each curve and turn, he has established a braking point or place where he should throw his car into a controlled drift. A break in his concentration can cause him to miss his point. The result is excessive braking, locked wheels, a spin. He's not out there alone. There are cars ahead and behind, sometimes bunched in heavy traffic, sometimes solitary, creeping up from behind or appearing suddenly in front with a blown engine, perhaps. He checks his mirrors regularly.

Although most of his time behind the wheel is spent shifting, steering, and generally adjusting his technique and line around the course to the traffic conditions, a driver checks his instruments at least once or twice on each circuit. Many drivers claim they can drive by the sound of the engine and use the tachometer only to attune their ear to the high-pitched whine or roar that signals a shift point. But the other instruments indicate the condition of one or more parts in their engine and transmission, and the driver relies heavily on them. An up-and-down fluctuation of the oil pressure can be a signal that more oil is needed. A sudden drop in the pressure is often a sign that something more serious is wrong. A drop in the oil pressure combined with a rise in the oil temperature is a good indication that a bearing is failing and causing improper lubrication, additional friction, and a sudden heat buildup. A rise in water temperature is a signal that something's wrong in the engine. Dropping fuel pressure is an indication of fuel starvation, a malfunctioning

161

pump, a valve problem, or a low fuel supply.

When a driver sees his car's temperature rise toward the end of a race, he may be able to bring it back down simply by dropping his engine speed a few hundred r.p.m. If he continues at maximum speed, his engine will overheat and fail, and he'll be forced out. By cutting his overall speed by a few miles per hour and his lap times by a few seconds, he can conserve his engine and finish the race.

Even though a lot of drivers have only a limited knowledge of the mechanical intricacies of their cars, most can interpret the readings they get in the cockpit and know how to adjust their driving to accommodate the engine. They also know when they must pull into the pits for a mechanic's attention.

With each circuit of the course, a driver can check on his progress and plan how he will handle the next lap. He can translate a pit

Top: *A nighttime pit stop at Daytona.* Below: *Jacky Ickx pours himself a drink before his turn at the wheel during the 1,000-kilometer race at Monza.* Opposite: *A pit stop at Le Mans by this privately entered Ferrari 512.*

signal reading "P-5 L-10 −18 +10" to "fifth place, ten laps remaining in the race, eighteen seconds behind the fourth-place car, and ten seconds ahead of the sixth." On the next circuit, he may see that he is still in fifth place, that there are nine laps remaining, but that he is now only sixteen seconds behind the fourth-place car. However, he is now only eight seconds ahead of the sixth-place car. Simple arithmetic tells him that if he keeps up this pace, he'll be able to pass the car ahead but will in turn be passed from behind. Without times, he's apt to relax his pace without realizing it. Although he might think he's driving his fastest, a slight, unconscious hesitation on a couple of corners can drop his times by a few seconds. By seeing his times on each lap, he can maintain a consistent pace and hunt for places on the track where he might do better.

Clear, cool weather is ideal for racing, but in sports car and Formula I racing, the show goes on regardless of the weather. The physical conditions on the track have to be taken very carefully into consideration by both drivers and mechanics. The driver adapts his technique to the track conditions; the mechanic alters the characteristics of the car as conditions change so that it continues to perform as well as possible.

If a course is tricky under normal, dry conditions, rain increases the danger on high-speed sweeping curves and long straightaways. In the dry the limits of a car are fairly definite. There's always a point at which the wheels will lock under braking and at which tires will slide under hard cornering. In the dry a driver can push his car right to that point

165

Opposite top and bottom: *Dusk on the Mulsanne straight, Le Mans, 1971.* Left: *Nighttime in John Wyer's pits at Sebring, 1971.* Below: *The Ferrari 512 of Mark Donohue and David Hobbs refuels at sunset, Sebring, 1971.*

and still have a certain margin for error. In the rain the limits of a car are indefinite, the margin for error, down to nothing. Cars traveling at high speeds over wet tracks have a nasty habit of aquaplaning—the car is traveling not on the asphalt but on the thin film of water that covers it. Unaware of that condition, a driver can easily lose control of his car.

Besides being unable to handle the car with the same confidence that he has in the dry, the driver can't see very well in the rain. The oversized rear tires with which cars are shod nowadays throw huge rooster tails of water into the air, a spectacular sight for the fans, but blinding to the driver in the following car. During the downpour at the 1970 Le Mans race, Reine Wisell of Sweden was headed slowly back to the pits in his Ferrari, unable to see through a windshield coated with oil and water. Suddenly, Italy's Clay Regazzoni, in another Ferrari, smacked into his rear. Mike Parkes, in still another Ferrari, rear-ended

Regazzoni, and Britain's Derek Bell completed the catastrophe by overrevving and blowing the engine in *his* Ferrari while trying to avoid the pileup. Rain had washed out the Italian marque in one soggy swoop.

To battle the problem of poor visibility, the Porsche 917s of 1970 and 1971 were equipped with a modified version of the wiper blades used on Boeing 707s. They helped, but not much. The major weapon with which the race driver combats slippery driving conditions are exotic tires that are designed to shed water quickly. The tread design of most of these rain tires is cast at the factory, but special patterns can be gouged from the tire right at the track with an electrically operated hand tool. There are endless arguments about the superiority of one type of rain tire or tread over another. American driver Mark Donohue,

after winning the opening race of the 1970 Trans-Am series during a cloudburst at Lime Rock, said that because of his Goodyear rain tires, he felt he almost had an unfair advantage over rival Parnelli Jones. Jones, under contract to Firestone, slid completely off the track on the very first lap.

The ability to drive in the rain is an art, and when the heavens open, there are one or two drivers who stand out as masters. These men would almost rather race in the rain, since their ability to control powerful cars in hazardous conditions gives them an immediate advantage. The late Pedro Rodriguez was renowned as a terror in the rain. As soon as the pavement turned wet, he gained on or pulled away from the opposition. Dicing with a car in the rainy BOAC 500-kilometer race at Brands Hatch outside London a few years ago,

Rodriguez passed it on the outside of Paddock Bend, a curve that has a dangerous reputation even in the dry. Vic Elford also is known for his ability in the wet.

One of the special skills I developed in rallying was the ability to drive fast in the wet, because in a rally the weather is generally not very good and you're driving on roads where it is icy or the adhesion is poor. The ability to drive in the rain followed me into racing. I can't say that I like driving in the rain. I don't think anyone enjoys it. Perhaps I dislike it less than most people. Unless you happen to be in front, you can't see anything. When you're trying to overtake a car all you see is a gigantic wall of water and spray. —V.E.

Long-distance endurance races, the 12- and 24-hour races such as Sebring, Daytona, and Le Mans, require sustained periods of night driving. Cars competing in these races are equipped with extremely bright driving lights so that drivers can continue through the darkness at speeds approaching their daylight speeds. The lights are usually mounted in sets of two. One set blazes far down the track, illuminating the long curves, while the other set throws a wider beam and lights up the long straights. Although these driving lights are far brighter than those on street cars, the blinding glare in the driver's eyes is less than on a highway since all the cars on the track are going in the same direction.

Few drivers mind racing at night; many actually prefer it to daylight driving since the track immediately ahead is the only thing lighted. There are no distractions in their field of view. Of course, those brilliant lights can go out suddenly. And rain at night is in many ways worse than during daylight. In the 1971 Sebring 12-hour race, Mark Donohue's Ferrari 512M had one of its lights knocked askew during a daylight shunt with Pedro Rodriguez's Porsche. Throughout the dark hours of the race one of his lights shone in the air at a 60-degree angle. One light lit half the track ahead; with the other he got a good view of the Martini Bridge and the Jaguar tower overhead but not much else.

The long night of a 24-hour endurance race takes on a dreamy, almost surreal atmosphere. At Daytona you can follow the progress of a car as its lights leap onto the first banking, shoot down the back straight, climb onto the second banking, flash by the grandstand, and then disappear along the infield. Spectators camping in the French countryside around the Le Mans circuit can hear the cars head down the three-and-a-half-mile Mulsanne straight, the drone of their engines like the sound of distant freight trains in the night. By the time one car has reached the end, another has started at the beginning—a long lullaby of differently pitched engines.

As night wears on in the garishly lit pits, mechanics catnap until the brightly colored cars, blackened now, limp in. Along the pits cars sit on jacks, their broad fiberglass tails in the air. Mechanics hover over damaged suspensions and sickly engines while drivers lounge or sleep on nearby cots. Everyone— drivers, mechanics, spectators—seems covered with a thin film of grime.

Teams backed by huge corporations or oil companies provide lavish trailers for their crews. Between stints at the wheel, their drivers can shower, sleep, and change into a clean suit. At Le Mans the Shell Oil Company has what amounts to a mini-hotel for the drivers it sponsors. Drivers can check into small rooms and be called by an attendant in time for their next turn on the track.

At Le Mans the hours of daybreak bring a new problem for drivers to cope with. Flying down the sections of the track that wind through the lush countryside, a driver comes on a fog bank or a patch of mist that hangs over the track. He has two alternatives—to pay no attention to it and blast through, hoping it's only a few yards deep, or to brake and carefully motor to the other side. The mist might extend down the track for several hundred yards, and if the driver bulls through, he'll be blind for seconds at 180 miles per hour. If he slows down and the fog continues for only a few yards, he loses time and feels foolish. On one lap the fog bank will be in one section of the track, but by the time the driver has completed the 8.2-mile circuit, it might have crept to another section of the track, enlarged, shrunk, or disappeared altogether. It's a totally random variable, something drivers don't like at all.

With the rising of the sun on a 24-hour marathon, a driver has the feeling that more than half the battle is over and a finish is near, a false feeling since both the 24-hour races, Daytona and Le Mans, start at 4 P.M. The morning light brings only another 7 or 8 hours of racing. By midmorning he's motoring around with fingers mentally crossed that his engine, his transmission, and his stamina will last until the afternoon. Along the length of the track, cars sit abandoned, broken, and wrecked. He shoots past without time to think about them, perhaps not wanting to.

It doesn't always work so smoothly, however. While winning the race is of great importance, drivers are not machines. Vic Elford remembers a moment during the morning of the second day of the 1972 Le Mans race.

By eight o'clock on Sunday morning, the race appeared to be virtually over. The Matras were in a commanding position. I think there were two Alfas left in the race, and they were running about fourth and sixth. There was one Lola still running, but it had been delayed during the night and was well back. Still, at that time on Sunday morning, it was going much quicker than anything else and was slowly catching the field. I had been in my car for about an hour and a half at that point and was beginning to feel that it wasn't too long before I'd be called in for my next fuel stop. I'd have a driver change with Helmut Marko and go off and have some breakfast.

At the end of the Mulsanne straight, Jo Bonnier, in the little Lola, passed me on the approach to the braking for the Mulsanne corner. As we came out of the corner, I was right behind him and followed him up the road through the long, fast curve going toward Indianapolis. The only other car in sight of us at that time, in front, was a Ferrari Daytona. I followed Jo, accelerating toward the Ferrari, and realized that he was going to try to overtake the Ferrari on the entrance to the next corner, not really a corner but a very fast swerve taken absolutely flat out by all the cars. I was in the unfortunate position of sitting there watching it, absolutely certain what was going to happen.

Start, right, and finish, below, signaled by flamboyant Tex Hopkins, of Watkins Glen six-hour race, 1971.

Then I saw the Ferrari and the Lola touch.

Jo seemed to realize at the last moment that he was making a mistake—that there wasn't room to get through—but at the same time, he was too close to be able to slow up and tuck in behind the Ferrari. He got off onto the grass with two wheels, touched the Ferrari at the same time, and the Lola then just spun and shot into the air like a helicopter. It spun through the trees before coming to rest some fifty to a hundred yards from the track. I hadn't seen the Lola going into the trees because as soon as the accident started, there was so much dust that both cars vanished. A few seconds later, I came through the dust cloud and found the Ferrari burning fiercely against the guard rail on the side of the track. I had no idea who the Ferrari driver was. I knew only that there was no signs of him. I thought that he might still be inside the car. Worse still, there was absolutely no sign whatsoever of the Lola or Jo Bonnier. I thought that possibly the Lola had gone into the air, come down on the other side of the Ferrari, and was possibly caught between the Ferrari and the guard rail. Jo would have been trapped inside.

There was nobody else around. There was nobody behind me. No other driver had seen the accident. My first thought was that Jo might be trapped under the Ferrari and that the driver in the Ferrari might also be trapped. I was much better equipped than anybody else to offer any kind of assistance because I was wearing my crash helmet and my full fireproof clothing. I stopped my car and rushed to the front of the Ferrari. There was still no sign of the Lola. I then went across and opened the door, looked into the Ferrari, and found to my surprise that there was nobody in it.

Only when I turned away in amazement, did I find that the driver had in fact been able to get out before I arrived and was already on the other side of the barrier. There was nothing I could do for Jo. He was very badly injured and died on the way to the hospital. After that, I didn't feel much like racing. I got back in the car and carried on until I was called in. Helmut Marko took over, and after a half an hour or so, the car retired with a broken gearbox.—V.E.

All professional drivers have had accidents during their careers. But as American driver Sam Posey said after seeing a film of his fiery crash at Riverside Raceway in California, "Drivers have to have a very short memory and very little imagination." During the 24-hour Daytona race several years ago, the late German driver Gerhart Mitter, driving a factory Porsche 908, slid in some oil dropped from a car with a blown engine and flipped onto his roof at close to 200 miles per hour. Amazingly, Mitter was completely unhurt; he walked back to his pits. Not wanting to give Mitter the time to reflect on this accident, the Porsche team manager called in another of the 908s and gave the car to Mitter, who not ten minutes before had been sliding wildly down the track upside down.

At today's speeds mechanical failure rather than driver error is the main cause of accidents. A vital strut breaking or a tire or engine blowing can change the handling of a car so violently and suddenly that there is no way a man can control his car. All he can do is hold on and hope. Mechanical failure was directly responsible for the deaths of three of the world's best in the recent past. Bruce McLaren, a top driver and designer, was killed when á new car he was testing suddenly veered off course at Goodwood, England. McLaren was far too good a driver to have lost control of his car that way. World champion Jochen Rindt, driving a Lotus Formula I, died when his car suddenly swerved sharply into the guard rail while he was practicing for the Grand Prix of Italy at Monza in 1970. And Pedro Rodriguez, a national hero of Mexico, died when his Ferrari suddenly lost a tire, hurling him into an embankment.

For every racing accident that results in bad injury or death, tragedies that people involved in racing don't talk about much, there are countless others that leave drivers with little more than a few cuts on the face, bruises here and there, and damaged pride. These are the accidents that drivers laugh about, at which they shake their heads in amazement— the car turned over, hit the wall, burned, flipped, burst apart, *but I survived.* Accidents that wreck more than one car are usually taken philosophically by the drivers. Leaping out of their flaming or otherwise badly damaged cars, they grin at each other, slap backs, and chalk it all up to bad luck. They are glad enough that they are out alive and not responsible, however remotely, for another's death or maiming. Occasionally, there is the shaking of a fist, and in at least one instance, drivers have come to blows.

The end of a bullfight, the end of a 100-yard dash or even the finish of an arm wrestling contest can be more visually evident than the end of a motor race. Through the hours the race has become a tangle of lap times, cars lapped and unlapped, and cars minutes

Below: *The winning Martini 917 is surrounded by a crowd after the finish at Le Mans, 1971.* Opposite: *Vic Elford signs an autograph after his win at the Nürburing, 1971.*

off the pace, yet everyone is moving around the track, passing and being passed. The casual spectator can have no idea of which car is being waved to victory when the checkered flag falls.

Sometimes the drivers get confused. A driver can think he's in the same lap with the winners, even that he's won the race, only to have the timekeepers tell him that he was a full lap behind. If his pit crew is alert, though, the driver is intensely aware, especially as the race nears its end, of just what his place is in the parade, and he has a good idea of just how much better he can do before the end.

In general, the longer the race, the greater the distance between the winning car and the rest. There are many cases when the winner was 30, 40, 100 miles ahead of the second-place car. But this isn't always the case. Because of its length, the 24 Hours of Le Mans has been called not a race at all; it's an endurance trial in which all that matters is finishing. Yet the end of the 1969 Le Mans may have been the most exciting finish of any motor race in history. After 23 hours of racing, the first- and second-place cars, Jacky Ickx in a Ford

GT-40 and Hans Herrmann in a Porsche 908, were still passing each other on every lap. On the final circuit, they were still dicing for the lead. Both cars appeared in view of the grandstands, at the same moment charging down to take the flag. At the very last turn, either could have taken it, and when they swept under the flag, Ickx had won by mere seconds.

The 1970 Grand Prix at Monaco produced another last-minute winner. Jack Brabham, in a car of his own make, had a fairly comfortable lead going into the closing laps, but Austrian Jochen Rindt in a Lotus was closing fast. On the final lap, Rindt was four seconds behind Brabham. As the two approached the last corner, a hairpin leading into the short start–finish straight, Rindt had closed the gap to only one second. Brabham came up on Piers Courage, in a slower car, and hesitated for a split second in deciding the side on which he should pass. In doing so he braked just beyond the last possible moment. His wheels locked, and he slid through the corner into the hay bales on the far side of the turn. Although only the nose of Brabham's car was damaged, by the time Brabham had backed up and headed for the finish line, Rindt had made the turn and crossed the line ahead of him. The starter was so surprised to see Rindt rather than Brabham appear around the corner that he neglected to give the Austrian the checkered flag. Holding the checkered flag in his hand, he just stared in amazement toward the corner where the luckless Brabham was untangling himself.

The checkered flag: In the popular mind, it's the ultimate symbol of winning.

And winning *is* what it's all about, isn't it? In Europe even more than in America, the fans cluster around the winning driver, pushing to be close to him, reaching out to touch him, hoping that something of his charmed life will attach to them. The winner's circle, with its champagne, girls, wreaths, huge trophies, and blown-up checks, is surely one of the most potent crucibles of drama that sport affords. At the end of the Dutch Grand Prix in 1970, world champion Jochen Rindt stood on the winner's platform surrounded by crowds, the band played the Austrian national anthem, and Rindt was wreathed in flowers. He stood, trying very obviously to hold back tears—he had learned moments before that one of his closest friends, Piers Courage, had been killed during the race.

Brian Redman has said that if you have driven a race as hard as you can and if you know you went to your own and the car's limit, you can feel satisfied at the end of the race whether you come in first or tenth or last. No one else is cheered like the winner, no one else receives the trophies and the adulation, but every driver in a race has put his life on the line. Everyone who finishes can be said to have entered into a contest with fear and won.

Still, it is the fastest man, whether by chance or skill, who is the symbol of that contest—the symbol of man's victory over high speed, flammable fuel, human fallibility, and yes, death.